The Good Financial Management Training Manual

Paul Palmer

Supported by

a member of
The Royal Bank of Scotland Group

National Mentoring Network

T000340

Published by NCVO Publications
National Council for Voluntary Organisations
Regent's Wharf
8 All Saints Street
London N1 9RL

© NCVO 2001

All rights reserved. No part of this publication may
be reproduced, stored in any retrieval system or
transmitted, in any form or by any means,
electronic, mechanical, photocopying or otherwise,
without the prior permission of the publisher.

A catalogue record for this book is available from
the British Library.

ISBN: 0 7199 1587 2

CONTENTS

	Page
Sponsor's Foreword	
Introduction	1

Chapter

1. Structuring the Organisation for Financial Strength	3
2. Financing the Mission	15
3. Budgeting	25
4. Resource Management	45
5. Special Financial Tools	65
6. Charity Accounts and Financial Management	85
7. Tax and Voluntary Organisations	97

ABOUT THE AUTHOR

Dr Paul Palmer BA Hons, PhD, FCIS, FIIA, is Head of the Centre for Charity and Trust Research and Director of Charity Courses at South Bank University, London. He is a trustee of the Royal Society of Health, the Friends of Southwark Cathedral and a member of the finance committee of Sargeant Cancer Care for Children.

ACKNOWLEDGEMENTS

I would like to thank my colleagues at South Bank University, David Wise, Stephen Williams and Ajjay Mandall for allowing me to use examples from their exam papers; Russell Moore at Saffrey Champness for his assistance on the tax chapter. Thanks also to the review panel and reference group set up by Maria Kane at NCVO, members of which provided valuable comments on the first draft:

Laurence Gandy, Director, North West Kent Council for Voluntary Service

R. Greyham Dawes, Director, Charities Unit, Horwath Clark Whitehill, Chartered Accountants

Andrew Robinson, Head of Community Development Banking, NatWest

Kate Sayer, Partner in Sayer Vincent, specialist charity auditors and advisers

Shirley Scott, Director, Charity Finance Directors Group

Catherine Wood, Head of Finance, NCVO

And a very special thanks to Neil Finlayson of haysmacintyre who reviewed the final draft.

Sponsor's Foreword

NOT FOR PROFIT/FOR PROFIT

>learning...
>all organisations require good financial management

>serving...
>it's not just about products and services
> tailored to the requirements of the sector

>adding...
>improving access to training and advice
> it's to our mutual benefit if you're sustainable and successful

>investing...
>with money ... and in other ways

>empathy...
>value driven with social objectives

Supporting this training manual is part of a process for NatWest. It's **community** investment – developing skills through advice and training; helping to make the most of limited resources. What we learn from the experience helps to shape the future of our work in the sector.

Andrew Robinson
Head of Community Development Banking
NatWest Bank plc

Supported by

a member of
The Royal Bank of Scotland Group

The Good Financial Management Training Manual

introduction

This book has been written as a practical companion to *The Good Financial Management Guide*, sponsored by NatWest, which was first published in 1999 to develop good practice in voluntary organisations. The guide was written in response to the widespread changes affecting the voluntary sector with its dramatic expansion, often funded by government, in the 1990s. Research indicated that some voluntary organisation financial management practices were lagging behind (GFMG, 1999). Trustees often lacked the financial information to make effective decisions within environments with a perceived increased risk as voluntary organisations moved from grants to contracts.

This training manual is designed to support the guide with practical work-based financial management exercises. The training pack can be used either as a self-learning text or by trainers. It is complementary to the guide and cross-references back to the guide where further explanation is required, particularly for accounting practices, legal, policy and management implications.

The Good Financial Management Training Manual follows the content structure of the guide. Each chapter begins with short introduction to the subject and reference to further reading in *The Good Financial Management Guide*. Practical exercises and examples are then provided. The manual is a practical training resource with exercises that require computation and evaluation leading to decision-making. Computational answers and suggested points for discussion are provided.

The book is primarily intended for charities with incomes ranging from £500,000 to £5 million. Examples and exercises are based at three levels of complexity:

- Introductory level: which test knowledge and comprehension;
- Intermediate level: which test application and analysis;
- Advanced level: which test evaluation and decision-making.

This format is intended to provide flexibility to a self-assessing reader or trainer who can therefore use the training pack by:

- tackling each subject chapter separately and working through all the examples, or

- just attempting those examples relevant to staff/trustees to have an overview at the appropriate level to their particular needs.

The training manual can be read and exercises attempted either individually or in groups. The discussion points provided at the end of the question and the suggested model answers are designed to allow participation. It is expected that the single reader/group will disagree with some of the suggested answers. The practical philosophy behind this manual takes the perspective that accounting and financial management is not a science or a 'value-free' neutral activity. There are various techniques and 'rules' to follow but interpretation and final decision-making is much more subjective. For example, if five people were to each win £1 million pounds on the lottery, they would all spend the money differently: some would spend immediately; others would look to invest for the longer term. Similarly voluntary organisations management committees and staff will have different priorities. Service delivery staff would probably like to increase resources immediately, finance staff to perhaps increase reserves, particularly if future funding is uncertain or there are projected cash flow problems. Fundraisers may want to see funds invested in technology or a new campaign. The final decision and the decision-making process is outside the scope of this manual. The manual does demonstrate the techniques that are used to compile the financial information which assists the decision-making process.

In 1995 a new Statement of Recommended Practice (SORP) for charities was introduced which provided an accounting framework for charities. The SORP has recently been revised and has focused on the importance of reporting. Essentially, the revised SORP evolves from financial accounting to a reporting statement requiring trustees to disclose more information about the organisation and in particular how they run it. An important aspect is the requirements for the trustees to undertake a risk assessment by stating what controls they have in place to reduce operational and financial risks.

The book has been written not just for the head of finance, finance officer or their staff, but for all those involved in voluntary action – the trustee, management team, staff and volunteers. The role of the voluntary finance officer has changed from bookkeeper to a provider of information going well beyond just the recording of transactions. Finance has become more complex; in particular, financial accounting information with its 'rules' and concepts of 'accruals' and 'depreciation' lead to questions such as: 'Where is the cash?' 'What do you mean it is restricted? They gave the money to the charity!' The answers leave many trustees and staff confused and often can lead to conflict and mistrust. It does not have to be like that!

Much financial accounting terminology applies to meeting the requirements of yearly published accounts and often has little bearing on daily decision-making, for example, how well you are doing against budget. Some 'rules of accounting' are relevant and with some practice can be understood. Accounting is essentially a very practical subject. In the same way you would not expect to drive a car without some prior training and certainly not take it on the road without learning the Highway Code, so it is with accounts and financial management. Much of the subject area of finance applied to voluntary organisations is simple to understand. It just requires a little practice – something this training pack will provide.

Paul Palmer

Chapter 1
structuring the organisation for financial strength

> **Objectives: By the end of this chapter you should understand:**
>
> 1. What is governance and its application to the voluntary sector
> 2. The link between governance and quality assurance
> 3. The role of the Voluntary Management Committee in financial management
> 4. The difference between financial monitoring, financial procedure and financial management.

GOVERNANCE

Governance can be defined as 'the system by which organisations are directed and controlled' (Cadbury, 1992). Many voluntary organisations are also charities and Section 97 of the Charities Act 1993 defines trustees as 'the people responsible under the charity's governing document for controlling the management and administration of the charity, regardless of what they are called'. Except in the smallest of charities and voluntary organisations the trustees will employ paid staff. The relationship between paid staff and trustees is crucial to an organisation's success. The seemingly simple question of who is responsible for authorising an element of expenditure can sometimes be fraught with difficulties and lead to internal strife, which only damages the organisation. (Guidance on the respective roles of trustees and chief officers has been provided by the Association of Chief Executives of Voluntary Organisations [ACEVO] – see useful addresses section at back of book).

Good governance is important for the voluntary sector for maintaining the confidence and financial support of the public. *The Good Financial Management Guide* (page 8) provides a checklist for voluntary organisations who wish to be clear and open about their work and conscious of their social responsibilities.

It is well established that there is a clear link between governance and quality assurance. A voluntary organisation's reason for existence is to deliver the best possible services to beneficiaries. However, sometimes it all goes wrong. It has been suggested that this happens because voluntary organisations lack the bottom line of profit and have to rely on softer, less quantifiable and measurable performance monitors and goals. These issues also confront the public sector and the search for value for money has often been linked to what have been termed the three 'E's – these can be defined for voluntary organisations as:

- Economic: not spending 95p to raise £1; essentially, minimising waste
- Efficient: getting the best use of what money is spent; a high output to input ratio

- Effective: spending funds so as to achieve the organisation's objectives; getting things done.

As we will illustrate later, performance measurement presupposes a good costing system. In recent years some funders have made a condition of their support a requirement for voluntary organisations to show that they have achieved and maintained, verifiable quality standards. *The Good Financial Management Guide* (page 10) outlines what a quality voluntary organisation should do. A discussion of the different models of governance, the recruitment of trustees and the role of the trustee board are discussed on pages 10-16 of the Guide.

THE FINANCIAL MANAGEMENT ROLE OF MANAGEMENT COMMITTEES

With the absence of a profit motive and shareholders, the financial management role of a voluntary organisation management committee is different from a commercial organisation. Principal differences are:

Accountability
Most voluntary organisations are financially accountable to a far greater number of stakeholders because they are funded by a combination of tax concessions and money from the general public, local government and charitable trusts.

Value
The goal of maximising shareholder value is not relevant to voluntary organisations. An alternative aim could be the maximising of public benefit as a voluntary sector goal. The management committee must demonstrate value for money and effectiveness. Shareholder value can be measured objectively through quantitative tools but Value for Money analysis has qualitative subjective criteria.

Three of the main functions of the Board are Financial Monitoring, Financial Procedures and Financial Management. *The Good Financial Management Guide* identifies the key points relating to the role of the Board in respect of each of these key functions.

Financial Monitoring

The financial monitoring carried out by Boards is often typified by:

- Comparing of budgets for income and expenditure with actual results
- Consideration of projected resources and levels of income and expenditure.

But its effectiveness can be limited by:

- The need to report to funders
- Being seen as a compliance function instead of seeking to add value

- Information which is too detailed and conforming to accounting regulations
- Totally reactive responses when information is presented.

Ideally, financial monitoring should be characterised by:

- The use of key financial ratio analysis (which can, for example, highlight financial stability)
- The inclusion of financial performance information against predetermined financial policies (for example, income reserves)
- A committee that is adequately empowered in its role by proper induction, an understanding of financial structures and its relationship with management
- The provision of information that is understandable, timely and accurate.

Financial Procedures

Procedures are designed to ensure the propriety and efficiency of the organisation's activities. The Board should ensure that there are proper policies and procedures governing:

- Trustees' financial responsibilities
- Controls on expenditure
- Controls on the financial assets
- Budgetary control
- Controls on human resources
- Controls on physical assets
- Controls on income generation.

A review of the accounting systems and related internal controls should be undertaken by the internal or external auditor who should report weaknesses in compliance and systems to the management committee.

Financial Management

Financial management is more than just ensuring there is sufficient cash and keeping to budget. Financial management involves:

- Setting financial objectives
- Planning and acquiring funds
- Ensuring funds are being effectively managed
- Management and financial accounting
- Formulating strategy
- Planning and controlling activities

- Decision-taking
- Optimising use of resources
- Disclosure to others external to the organisation
- Disclosure to employees
- Safeguarding assets.

Clear procedures are needed to ensure that the management board has the skills to ensure effective financial management takes place. Where staff are involved the individual responsibilities should be clear to avoid 'stepping on each other's toes'. The role of the honorary treasurer or a chair of a finance committee is often crucial in discussions with key financial external advisors – investment managers, auditors etc. Other board members must, however, recognise that they hold a joint responsibility and must not assume the honorary treasurer will do everything.

ACTION POINTS FOR YOUR ORGANISATION

'Audit' your organisation by checking to see if you have:

1. **A clear procedure for the election, times served and retirement of Board members?**

2. **Undertaken an assessment of the requirements and type of skills you wish for the management committee?**

3. **A procedure to record conflicts of interest that may arise for Board members?**

4. **Undertaken regular self-assessment of the organisation: Is it carrying out its mission effectively; appraisal of the chief executive's performance; reviewed the Board's performance – its strengths and weaknesses?**

5. **Timely and effective management information to assist with control?**

6. **A financial procedure manual? Does it have clear rules on the authorisation of expenditure, cheques signing authority etc?**

7. **A Board which is proactive in financial management with a plan for longer-term objectives?**

8. **A job description for the Honorary Treasurer or terms of reference for the finance committee?**

9. **An annual 'management letter' from the external auditors?**

Further explanation and illustrative examples to support the above are found in chapter one of The Good Financial Management Guide.

WHAT HAVE WE LEARNT?

Questions: Answers are in the text or referenced to in The Good Financial Management Guide. Have a go before looking at them.

1. How is 'Value for Money' defined?

2. What should a quality voluntary organisation be able to demonstrate?

3. What are the two principal financial differences between a commercial organisation and a voluntary organisation?

4. What are the ideal financial monitoring characteristics of a voluntary board?

5. List five key controls that should be contained within a financial procedures manual?

CASE STUDY 1.1

'Mind Craft' trust was founded five years ago by a senior art therapist – John Thurstrom – who was concerned that the artistic output of people who had mental health problems was not being displayed in commercial art galleries. John, himself an artist, set up the charity to be a 'clearing house' and advocate between artists who had mental health problems and the commercial art galleries, which sell their work. John formed a committee of trustees, of direct friends and their friends, which included prominent artists who did not have mental health problems, a leading gallery owner and respective partners in top firms of accountants and solicitors. John was the chair of the trust, which had no paid staff.

John continued to work as an art therapist but after two years explained to his fellow trustees that the charity was not going to get anywhere unless there was some full-time staff. John was due for a year's paid sabbatical – to write a book – and proposed to his fellow trustees that he would also spend more time on developing the trust. During the year John's energy and enthusiasm transformed the trust, which obtained some contracts with commercial art galleries, receiving a commission of 25% on the sale of each picture as a fee. It also received a substantial donation from a wealthy individual and a grant from a trust. At the end of the first year the trust's income was £250,000 with some five staff in London (in John's house) and a network of volunteer agents/staff spread throughout the country.

John proposed to his fellow trustees that he should continue working for the trust and had arranged a further year's sabbatical – unpaid – from his employers. The trustees agreed that he should continue in this role and remain as 'executive chairman'. The solicitor trustee advised that she would write to the Charity Commission telling them of this decision and seeking their approval as John would be paid.

The trust continued to grow, doubling its income by the end of the year. John then proposed to the trustees that he should step down and the trust should appoint a chief executive. 'After all', he said, 'I still have my book to write!' A chief executive was subsequently appointed who in turn appointed new staff and a new London Head office was acquired. Six months into the job at a meeting of the trustees, the chief executive explained that the organisation's business plan – which had been drawn up by John – was totally unrealistic. Growth of income to a million pounds was unsustainable as it was based upon verbal, unconfirmed promises and expectations.

Staff and volunteers were exhausted and some artists were complaining about the 25% commission the trust took. One artist had contacted The Guardian newspaper which had sent a reporter round and said that commercial agents' normal fees were 10%. John replied that the very nature of a voluntary organisation was to be pioneering and adventurous, otherwise it would never start. Secondly the higher commission fee was based on promoting the trust and its vision. The chief executive's view was that it would have been a good idea to tell the artists. Vision was fine but business sense also had to be applied.

Following the meeting, the chief executive submitted his resignation 'with immediate effect'. The trustees met and John explained that he had negotiated a further leave of absence and would again 'manage the organisation' until the current problems were resolved.

> **Questions**
>
> 1. What are your observations on the governance of the organisation?
>
> 2. What different actions the trustees could have taken?
>
> 3. What actions should the trustees take now?

CASE STUDY 1.2

People concerned with the use of chemicals in food production had founded the Association for Agricultural Advancement in the early 20th century. The Association had grown to over 10,000 members by the middle of the 1970s but membership had since declined to 7,000 members by the beginning of the year 2000. The trustees of the Association met six times a year and consisted of 45 members who were elected from a variety of different professional interests. For much of the 20th century the Association's income had come from membership fees and examination fees from its qualification in nutritional management. In 1998 the Association found that its qualification had been superseded by university qualifications and that income from registration and examination fees which had once been 70% of the income was now closer to 40% (some £400,000) in 2000 and still declining at the rate of 10% per year.

The Association produced a quarterly journal and held lectures for its members whose fees had not increased since 1989 – in part to stem the loss in membership. This had only been partially successful as membership continued to decline by 250 per year. Fees are £85 per annum. However, the annual expenditure exceeded the annual income and the substantial reserves the Association had built up in earlier years of £700,000 were being drawn down quite quickly. Some good news and potential for the Association was the interest in organic food. Two of the trustees were experts in this area and they had proposed a new qualification.

The trustees in 2000 had appointed a new chief executive and director of finance. To support them and to 'manage the crisis' a new committee structure had been agreed at the Annual General Meeting which had abolished all the former committees and replaced them with a smaller executive committee which met monthly. The full trustee meeting was to be half-yearly. The new honorary treasurer, chair and deputy chair formed the executive with the chief executive and finance director. The new executive set about their role with enthusiasm, particularly the Honorary Treasurer who regularly visited the organisation. With the finance director they reviewed financial procedures and introduced cost-cutting measures. Over half the staff in the education department that administered the qualification had been made redundant at a one-off cost of £150,000, leaving an ongoing annual expenditure for the year 2000 of £1.2 million.

At the next trustee meeting, the member who edited the journal complained that writers for the journal who received a fee of £50 per annum had either not been paid or found that tax had been deducted. She explained that her job was becoming impossible as people were upset by such 'shabby treatment' and were refusing to write for the journal. One member pointed out that the journal was now the only 'benefit' members received. A former chairman now retired who came down from Scotland to the meetings in London claimed that his expenses had not been paid because his tea receipt for 95 pence had not been attached. Three months later he was still waiting for payment despite sending it back saying that the Association could have the 95p. He went on to say that the fare was in excess of £100, which he had personally incurred and that, as a pensioner, this was money he could ill afford.

The Honorary Treasurer replied that the Association was in financial crisis and that all expenditure had to be monitored. He personally checked all expense claims. The writers for the journal had not been paid, as they had not sent in proper invoices or a letter from their tax offices, which confirmed that they were self-employed for tax purposes. He had taken advice from the auditors on freelance staff and they had advised him that tax had to be deducted.

One member explained that he had not realised how desperate the situation had become. They asked how long the Association had to survive? Were they protected from personal liability if the organisation were to become insolvent? Another member said the treasurer deserved everyone's support for his hard work. One of the experts in organic food asked if there had been any progress made on the new qualification? Heated discussions followed before the questions of 'How long have we got?' and 'What plans were there to get us out of this problem?' were put to the chairman. As the chair turned to the chief executive, the Treasurer interjected: 'I am working on these figures at the moment and it would be inappropriate to answer this question until the executive committee has discussed them'.

Questions

1. **Estimate the current financial situation of the Association and how long has it got before reserves are exhausted (assuming cost inflation of 3 per cent per annum on expenditure but no increase in exam fees or membership subscriptions)?**

2. **Is the Treasurer correct in the advice on the payment to the writers?**

3. **Is the Treasurer's conduct and current role appropriate?**

4. **Critically evaluate the current management of the organisation and make suggestions as to how they could improve it.**

ANSWERS TO CASE STUDIES

These draft answers are designed as discussion points. As with all case studies there is no definitive answer. However, from the financial management and governance perspective they illustrate points of best practice.

Case Study 1.1

1. There is potential confusion between John's role as chairman, founder and employee. The trustees sought Charity Commission permission for his paid role. If they agree to his again taking over they will have to do so again unless the constitution had been changed.

2. Founders who then become chief executives and back to chairs have a potential conflict with a new chief executive. The other trustees could have appointed a different chair from John to avoid such conflicts.

3. Imposing a business plan as ambitious as this one on a new chief executive by the chair would inevitably lead to conflict. The trustees should have recognised that a conflict would arise. They should have provided a mechanism to review the business plan that would have depersonalised the review. The Honorary Treasurer, for example, could have chaired and presented the revised business plan.

4. The organisation's vision has clearly not been communicated and the organisation's accountability to its beneficiaries is confused. Whereas corruption is probably not an issue, the potential for exploiting the users is real. Equally, poor communication could lead to embarrassing publicity. Has the charity made clear in its literature and contracts with artists that it charges a higher commission? Why does it charge that amount and has it got the commitment of its supporters to this policy?

5. John is clearly highly committed to the organisation but now needs to take a step back. The trustees, if they agree to John's offer of managing the organisation again, need to have a clear exit route for John and a succession plan.

Case Study 1.2

The Association has an annual income this year of:

Fees £85 x 7,000 =	£595,000
Exams	£400,000
Total Income	£ 995,000
Expenditure	£1,200,000
Redundancy	£150,000
Deficit	£ 355,000
Reserves	£700,000
Balance on Reserves	£345,000

Next Year

Fees £85 x 6,750 =	£573,750
Exams £400,000 less 10% =	£360,000
Total Income	£ 933,750
Expenditure (3% inflation increase)	£1,236,000
Forecast Deficit	£302,250
Reserves brought forward	£345,000
Balance on Reserves	£42,750

1. The Association has just over two years of reserves without changing its expenditure pattern or allowing for interest on its balances.

2. Yes. Unless there is clear evidence that the writers are self-employed or they have signed the appropriate declaration form, tax should be deducted. However, if tax is to be deducted this should be communicated to the writers before they carry out any work.

3. The treasurer has become confused and is acting more like a financial controller than the honorary treasurer. What is the job of the finance director? The honorary treasurer has become too involved in day-to-day matters instead of taking a strategic vision and facilitation role.

4. The organisation has clearly not thought through its governance: petty disputes, i.e. withholding payment while sorting out 95 pence. The Council only meeting half-yearly will lead to divisions and hostility at a time when it should be pulling together. Not giving or having the financial information to hand and sharing it, given the nature of charity trusteeship as a joint liability, is counterproductive. The executive are not different from their fellow trustees. Whereas 45 trustees making decisions is too many, changing suddenly to three trustees has gone to the other extreme and communication is clearly breaking down.

5. The Association has adopted a 'knee jerk' reaction to its problem and turned it into a crisis. It needs to take a strategic view of its future. It has some time and opportunities to develop a new income stream. By making the staff redundant, has it lost the capacity to take advantage of this opportunity?

Chapter 2
financing the mission

> **Objectives: By the end of this chapter you should understand:**
>
> 1. The link between objectives, goals and action plans
> 2. The complementary nature of organisational mission and finance
> 3. Applying strategic evaluation and its application
> 4. Planning within a quality framework.

DEFINING THE MISSION

Voluntary organisations should be clear as to why they exist and how they will fulfil their mission. This may seem obvious but many voluntary organisations become confused over why they exist and how they plan to fulfil their mission. Meeting a financial goal is not the mission of a voluntary organisation but is essential if it is to fulfil its mission. For example, in the case of the ambitious campaign by the NSPCC on child abuse, the mission is to eradicate cruelty to children but to achieve it requires £200 million. Aspirations and financial resources are related and it is the task of managers to co-ordinate the two.

Financial planning for voluntary organisations can be thought of as a cycle of related charitable and financial concerns as shown in Figure 1:

Figure 1

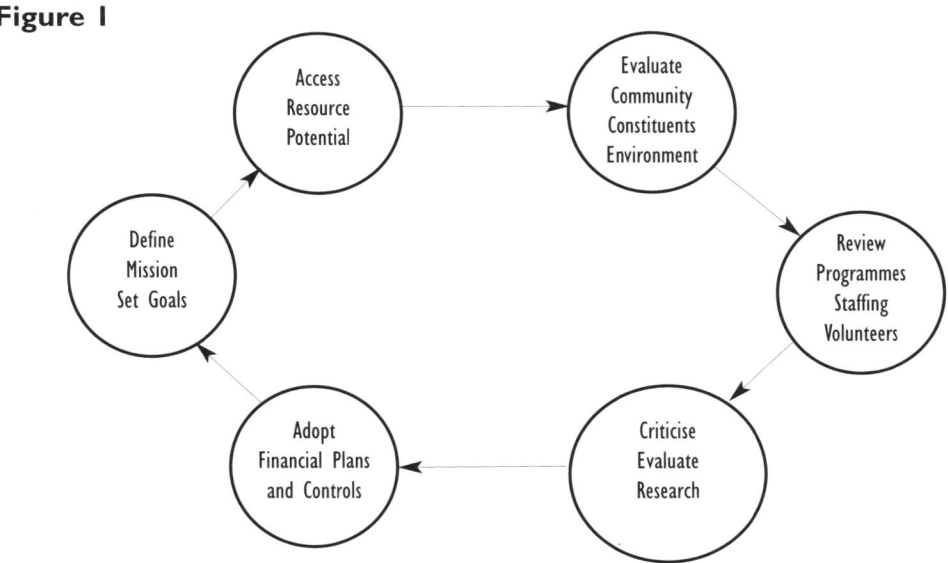

Source: The Good Financial Management Guide p31

A voluntary organisation mission and its financial goals are complementary to each other, not in competition.

PLANNING

Planning can be defined as the establishment of objectives and the formulation, evaluation and selection of the policies, strategies, tactics and action required to achieve these objectives. Planning comprises long-term strategic planning and short-term operations planning, which is usually for up to one year. Voluntary organisations need to plan effectively but often do not because:

1. In many voluntary organisations, the demands of the moment – fire-fighting, meeting income targets and controlling expenditure – leave little time for strategic analysis.

2. Too little is known about how complex external factors affect voluntary organisations.

Planning really happens in three stages:

1. Deciding general goals
These are usually long-term aims to pursue and tend to be set at top levels. Using the WWF-UK Strategic Development Plan this would be: 'To seek to slow down, and eventually to reverse, the destruction of species and habitats throughout the world'.

2. Setting objectives
Within the context of general goals, objectives are set as clear steps on the way to achieving the goals. They are statements of specific measurable results to be achieved in a given time. For example WWF-Scotland has the opportunity through the Scottish Parliament to advocate its community-based participatory approach to conservation. For its core costs WWF-Scotland will continue to seek funds as part of WWF-UK but its programme expenditure will be increasingly sourced from within Scotland.

Although objectives are set within the context of the goals set at the top, they also depend on information from the bottom up, to ensure they are feasible.

3. Action plans
These are detailed plans of how the goals and objectives are to be achieved, using information from those who will carry out the task. In respect of the objective of WWF-Scotland sourcing project finance from Scotland its action plan in respect of the activities of research might state:

- Conduct 10 pieces of research, 70 per cent of costs of which will be funded from Scottish sources;

- Publish six pieces of research this year, 60 per cent of costs of which will be funded from Scottish sources.

Understanding the strategic position

To answer the question 'What is, or will be, our strategic position?' requires an organisation to understand the external environment in which it operates, as well as its own internal structures. This has four aspects:

1. Environmental analysis (external appraisal) is the scanning of the organisation environment for factors relevant to the organisation's current and future activities. To assist this process NCVO has developed a 'Third Sector Foresight' project which seeks to understand these external factors and how they impact on the sector.

2. Position audit examines the current state of the entity in respect of resources both financial and organisational, for example, the qualities of the management committee.

3. Organisational appraisal (or SWOT analysis) is a critical assessment of the strengths, weaknesses, opportunities and threats in relation to the internal and environmental factors affecting an entity in order to establish its position prior to the preparation of a long-term plan.

4. Gap analysis arises from a projection of current activities into the future to identify if there is a difference between the organisation's objectives and the results from the continuation of current activities.

Undertaking this assessment helps to identify the strategic choices open to the organisation, for example, to grow or to stay the same size or even reduce in size; issues of current and future service provision, geography and policy. To assist this process *The Good Financial Management Guide* (page 36) recommends a number of techniques.

Evaluation

Once choices are identified they need to be evaluated as it is unlikely that all options will be feasible within available resources. Each option should be examined on its merits as to whether it:

- Increases strengths
- Strengthens existing weaknesses
- Is suitable to the organisation's existing position
- Is acceptable to stakeholders.

In addition, in testing their feasibility the following questions should be asked:

- Is the leadership suitable?
- Is the culture capable?
- Is the organisational structure appropriate?
- Are the functional policies appropriate?

- Are the resources available?
- Is this strategy an improvement on not changing at all?
- Are there procedures for implementation and monitoring?

Each chosen strategy needs to satisfy all these points. If it fails on any, the organisation must assess whether remedial action is possible.

Preparing day-to-day plans

Once the strategic goals have been identified they must be translated into day-to-day activities. For example, a cancer charity aiming to reduce the incidence of smoking might set an objective to reduce smoking in women attending antenatal clinics by 25 per cent within the next six months. To achieve this objective the following action plans have been formulated:

- a pamphlet explaining the dangers
- a counselling session
- a chance to attend an anti-smoking course.

The action plan for producing the pamphlet may be further broken down into a number of tasks as follows:

- Identify major issues, medical and otherwise, of which expectant mothers should be aware

- Identify main contributors to pamphlet

- Prepare draft, check accuracy of content and design

- Conduct a limited testing with readers'/users' panel

- Print

- Market and promote pack to expectant mothers attending the clinics.

The persons responsible for each of these tasks, and the time allocated, should be identified, so as to provide a basis for performance appraisal.

Planning within a quality framework

A quality framework makes possible a rigorous and consistent approach to quality throughout an organisation. In *The Good Financial Management Guide* the work of the Quality Standards Task Group is discussed (page 38) and an Excellence Model is outlined that can be applied to any organisation.

PROGRAMME AND ORGANISATIONAL RESOURCE ASSESSMENT

Mission-orientated goals and financial goals are interdependent. Any change that improves or gives a new strategic direction to charitable programmes will also mean an adjustment to the financial resources devoted to that programme. For example:

A voluntary organisation providing counselling services decides to increase the number of its qualified counsellors. The education department, which runs the training course, responds by planning to increase its intake by 20 per cent next year. In planning this expansion there will be implications for changes in the number of tutors, teaching rooms, equipment, administration etc which will need to be costed. In addition to these changes, the budget for the training department must include an allowance for the likely changes in the price of relevant items during the budget period, salaries etc.

Often a voluntary organisation is faced with a situation where the committee has to prioritise options, as it does not have sufficient resources. In drawing up a list of possible solutions the link between mission and financial resources should be explicit and a criterion rating each solution as viable or unacceptable can be used. For example, the Royal Society for the Promotion of Health in reviewing its Annual Lecture notes that it constantly makes a loss and considers the option of increasing income by seeking sponsorship. Its mission is to promote health awareness and therefore to accept sponsorship from a tobacco company would not be acceptable, no matter how attractive the financial offer.

Voluntary organisation management committees also need to consistently consider their organisations' financial stability. The longer-term planning includes assessing the stability of sources of finance and their impact on reserve levels etc. This is referred to as 'organisational resource analysis' and an example of this is outlined in *The Good Financial Management Guide* on page 42.

ACTION POINTS FOR YOUR ORGANISATION

'Audit' your organisation by checking to see if it has:

1. **A mission statement** that is relevant and understood throughout the organisation and by its stakeholders

2. **A strategic plan with goals and objectives**

3. **A planning process that corresponds to the quality framework**

4. **Action plans with clear responsibilities**

5. **Performance measurement linked to the action plans**

6. **A management committee which** undertakes regular performance and organisational resource assessment.

WHAT HAVE WE LEARNT?

Questions: You will find the answers are in the text or referenced to in The Good Financial Management Guide. Have a go before looking at them.

1. Draw the financial planning cycle.

2. What are the stages of planning?

3. Outline the four aspects of understanding a strategic position.

4. In evaluating an organisation, what are the factors that need to be examined?

5. What additional questions need to be asked of a chosen strategy?

6. Describe the proposed planning quality principles for a voluntary organisation.

EXERCISE:

SAMPLE EXERCISE

Happy Homes has two properties, which provide short-term residential accommodation for disabled people in the Bristol City area thereby allowing those who care for them to have a holiday. The finance director says: 'We plan to raise more money to allow us to build more homes – we expect to borrow at a good rate – which will enable us to give more people who look after their relatives a break. After all, we've promised our supporters a 10 per cent increase in places available and we do not want to break our word.'

Identify the organisational, business and functional strategies in the above quotation.

Suggested answer

The organisational objective is to expand its service to support people who care for others. The organisational strategy is the decision that this will be achieved by building new homes rather than, say, diversifying into day support. The business strategy suggests that this be best achieved by building new properties rather than extending current properties. The operational strategy involves the decision to invest in new properties (the service function) which is to be financed by loan finance (the finance function) rather than seeking funds from government or the public.

EXERCISE 2.1

You have recently been appointed as the finance and administration director of an ethnic minority national membership-based organisation which co-ordinates local groups. The organisation has an income from various sources of £1.2 million. The chief executive has been asked by the management committee to organise its first business planning exercise following a critical report on the organisation by a major funder. They ask for your help.

Prepare a briefing note for the chief executive and the three other senior managers outlining the topics which should be covered in the business planning process and advising them on who should be included in the business planning team.

CASE STUDY 2.2

The Emergency Support Service is now faced with a changing environment. ESS was founded in 1974 following local government re-organisation to provide volunteers for social services. In the past ESS was funded entirely by national government on a grants basis. The grant was increased in line with inflation every year.

The last government believed a central incremental grant encouraged inefficiency. The government introduced a tapering reduction in grant of £1 million per year (the ESS budget was then £6 million) and required ESS instead to tender to individual local authorities for its services on a contract basis. Local authority contracts are increasingly being awarded to local voluntary organisations, particularly in Scotland and Wales or other national charity competitors, for example, the Women's Royal Voluntary Service and the British Red Cross in England who undercut ESS prices. In addition ESS is faced with a general freeze on government spending in accordance with the new government's commitment to keep within borrowing limits and the previous government's expenditure plans. ESS has a budgeted contingency reserve of one year's current expenditure and has a remaining 20-year lease on its London headquarters.

Discuss

Appraise the situation of the ESS and recommend appropriate strategies to deal with its problems.

ANSWERS TO EXERCISES/CASE STUDIES

Exercise 2.1

The note to the chief executive should cover:

1. The reason or rationale for having a business plan
For example: to set down effective criteria for improving the organisation's performance through a process of planning and evaluation.

2. The objectives of a plan

3. The main components of a business plan, normally:
a) The organisation's mission including the extent to which the organisation's values have changed over time and how should this be reflected in what the organisation does
b) Internal and external appraisal
c) Environmental assumptions
d) Clear objectives, ideally quantified
e) Strategy (including marketing)
f) Budgets
g) Performance measures to demonstrate efficiency and effectiveness of the organisation
h) Feedback system.

4. The staff involvement in the process
All the organisation's senior mangers and the management committee should be involved in the business planning process, not just simply to approve it, but also to own the strategy. While the senior managers will develop the business plan all the organisation will be involved and therefore will know what is expected of them. This will mean that a hierarchy of objectives and delegated responsibilities from the management committee to operational staff will exist. A failure to involve operational staff and management committee members will result in confusion and a loss of direction.

Case Study 2.2

1. Situation appraisal
ESS is not in a good position. It has seen its reliable source of income disappear and is now exposed to new and growing competition in a static market. ESS has moved from having one 'customer', central government, to having some 400 new customers throughout the country. Viewed as a 'London English' organisation it is unlikely to have developed regional structures, marketing skills or commercial acumen. It probably lacks a proper costing system.

2. A strategic plan would have to take the following factors into account:

a) The competitive environment is hostile with a static market and geographical problems; there are new competitors and barriers of entry for new competitors have been abolished. It is not all bad news. ESS is now free to consider tendering to health authorities.

b) The political environment is unlikely to restore the ESS central grant. Government spending plans indicate that there will be an increase in public sector spending – particularly in the health sector – but not at present. It is not feasible for ESS with limited reserves and assets to undertake a sort of holding operation in the expectation that funding and new markets will increase.

c) The economic environment predicts low levels of inflation except in London where ESS is based and here wage inflation has outstripped national levels reflecting the higher cost of living. Low levels of inflation also indicate that contract funds are unlikely to increase. Local and health authorities will seek to maximise the lowest economic cost. For the voluntary sector economy the increase in funding to the sector has come from government or trading activities. Donations from the public and business have been static. ESS has no expertise in raising funds from the general public or corporations.

d) The competitive environment is not likely to diminish with national and local competitors. ESS has major problems with its geographical position in dealing with the devolving of power to Scotland and Wales.

3. The organisation structure and culture of the ESS

a) ESS had been reliant on just one source of finance in a very cosy relationship. This has not prepared it for the rigours of the new contract environment. ESS probably has few marketing skills as it has never had to tender for contracts. Trustees would have been appointed for their 'name' and prestige in government or the voluntary sector. As the organisation has never really had a marketing objective it does not have the experience in its paid staff or trustees to re-orientate itself. At the same time it still does have contact with government and a tapering arrangement which might enable it to 'buy' more time to equip itself with those skills.

b) It is possible that the services provided by ESS were organised according to central government specifications. Local government is free to decide on its own service provision and may not have the same priorities. Having been a monopoly supplier with a distinct culture of one type of service delivery this may not be relevant for all local authorities.

c) The one grant a year has meant that the accounting system has not previously priced contracts. It could be that the organisation has no real idea of how much a particular service costs and what should be the contribution to organisational overheads. Losing contracts on price to other national competitors would indicate that there is something wrong with the way ESS prices. On the other hand it may be that other competitors are larger and so benefit from economies of scale; or that ESS is inefficient and lacks proper project management skills.

4. Strategic options available to ESS

a) Expand into the health service market. This may not be easy as ESS has no relationships or background with health authorities. Existing service suppliers will be hostile to ESS.

b) Develop new services. This is easier said than done as ESS has been a single service organisation. Does it have the skills to develop new services and are these services which local and health authorities would need?

c) ESS could develop a more aggressive pricing policy. It still has a government grant covering some core costs.

d) Change the accounting system for more accurate and relevant cost information.

e) ESS could make itself more efficient by rationalisation.

f) A long-term strategic option would be to assess the need for volunteers, particularly in caring for people who wish to stay in their own home rather than go into residential care. ESS could set itself up as a specialist operator in keeping people at home and charge wealthier people a fee.

g) The competitive static market with increasing costs might lead to ESS considering sharing its resources with other voluntary organisations. Alternatively it may have skills in training and supporting volunteers that it could provide to smaller voluntary organisations. ESS could set up joint ventures with other voluntary organisations.

h) If ESS, having reviewed its options, fails to come up with a viable plan, or the plans it develops requires resources which the organisation does not have, then it should consider merging with another voluntary organisation. This would preserve jobs and the commitment and skills of volunteers.

Chapter 3
budgeting

> **Objectives: By the end of this chapter you should understand:**
>
> 1. What the purpose of a budget is
> 2. How to prepare forecasts and use forecasting techniques
> 3. The importance of cash budgets
> 4. The objectives of budgetary control
> 5. The advantages of flexible budgeting methods over fixed budgets.

WHAT IS BUDGETING?

A budget is a plan translated into money for a defined period of time. The time period is usually one year. The budget is prepared after the organisation has clarified its aims and objectives and produced a variety of action plans to achieve them. The purposes of a budget are:

1. To co-ordinate different activities (departments) towards a single plan
2. To communicate and set targets
3. To maximise and allocate resources
4. To identify financial problems
5. To establish a system of control by having a plan against which actual results can be compared
6. To compel planning.

Budget Planning

Setting a budget involves translating plans into pounds (or euros). Parts of the plan can be calculated with precision whereas other aspects are more a matter of estimation. Before calculation can take place a number of key decisions will have to be made. These include:

Balancing
Does the budget have to be balanced, that is, one that aims to produce no surplus or loss? Such a decision will have other implications for the financial management of the charity in relation to the level of reserves the organisation holds and, if a deficit is planned implications for the liquidity, and the cash flow of the organisation, will it be able to pay salaries?

Timing
Budgets must be completed to a deadline. This includes ensuring that the

timing matches the decision-making process of funders. Realistic dates also need to be set to allow those contributing to the budget and those doing the calculations and co-ordination (the finance person or department) sufficient time to complete their tasks.

Evolution

During the year events can occur which cause or require a radical change. Budgets can then become unrealistic or inaccurate. Budgets can and should be changed to reflect new circumstances, otherwise in an original or unaltered state they could continue to signal a problem even though it has been resolved. An alternative is to keep the original budget but provide a note explaining the changes. However, this course of action can be ineffective for monitoring and control purposes. An alternative is to set up a flexible budget system, which is explained on page 63 of *The Good Financial Management Guide*.

Accountability – allocating responsibility

The planning process will have helped to clarify who has the power to affect various parts of the budget. As far as possible, action plans will only have been provided by those who carry responsibility for delivering the service and the general rule is to push the financial authority down to that level. For example, a drug rehabilitation charity may have decided to cut the number of places it offers in hostels by providing more help through detached support workers to people in their own homes. The detached workers co-ordinator would have been consulted as to the feasibility of extending services and an extra cost agreed. The co-ordinator then becomes a budget holder, responsible for providing the agreed level of service within that cost.

Zero based versus incremental basis

Many budgets are drawn up yearly by simply applying a percentage increase to the items originally agreed. This is referred to as 'incremental' budgeting. This method is criticised as it fails to consider whether activities and costs are still relevant and whether the amount allocated is still appropriate. It also does not recognise inefficiency, and mistakes in one year will continue to be repeated. An alternative is to assess every budget item as if it was now. This method is called 'zero-based' budgeting. In practice, incremental budgeting is the most widely used. This is because many items and activities, particularly in service-providing voluntary organisations, are so fundamental to the organisation that they will continue each year, especially if they are contract-funded. In addition, to review every line item would require so much time and cost that it would be self-defeating as the net cost saving would probably be minimal. This is not to say that you should dismiss zero-based techniques. What you should do, as part of your overall management activities, is to review your activities regularly.

Types of Budget

Budgets should be drawn up according to the needs of the organisation. The basic budget is an estimate of incomes and expenditures for the forthcoming year. A relatively simple financial organisation with a few sources of income and one expenditure activity may just require one budget. More financially complex organisations will require a master budget, which is supplemented by a series of budgets on different activities created to meet specific planning and assessment needs. These will range from departmental-type budgets, which will be amalgamated to form the master budget, or different types of budgets – for example, projections on the cash needs of the organisation or the capital (longer-term) needs.

Advantages, disadvantages and participation

The Good Financial Management Guide (pages 59-60) provides coverage of these topics. The important points to note are:

- An organisation without a budget for the year ahead is unlikely to survive, unless its reserves are significant.

- The budgeting process is a facilitation tool to support the aims of the organisation; it is not in itself a purpose and must not stifle the creativity of the organisation.

- Participation, particularly if it's 'bottom-up', is vital to a budget's success.

Budget Scheduling and Manuals

Budgeting in most organisations is a cyclical activity revolving around the financial year with:

1. Finance department/officer providing a plan and budget worksheets some six months before the budget is due to start to budget holders.

2. Budget holders will then compile the respective budget for their activity and return to the finance officer responsible.

3. The finance officer responsible will then combine all the budgets and create a master budget, which the chief executive (management team in larger organisations) will then review and seek approval by the management committee.

In smaller voluntary organisations this activity is usually informal. Larger more complex organisations, particularly with branches, may have a more formal procedure usually outlined in a budget manual, a formal written document that explains the purpose of the budget, the formal procedures and time frame to be followed (see pages 61-62 of *The Good Financial Management Guide* for more information). In addition, the manual could also cover the issues of meeting a particular funder's requirements and whether or not budgets can be changed.

Many voluntary organisations are dependent on just one source of income. In service delivery organisations this may be a statutory funder and in such cases the voluntary organisation is well advised to follow the format of the funder. If this format is not suitable for control purposes, the organisation can use a spreadsheet to convert its accounts into the funders' format. It is important to keep a clear trail and reconciliation between the two different documents. If such exercises are required they should be viewed as a compliance cost of meeting the needs of funder.

A common misconception about budgets is that once set they cannot be changed. In part this comes about because the term 'fixed budget' is used by cost accountants. The term 'fixed budget' actually means that budget has been prepared on one estimate of income and expenditure at one level of activity. For example, an advice service will see 100 people a week or a hostel will be 80 per cent occupied. Unforeseen events can occur which are beyond an organisation's control. Should the budget then be changed to reflect these changed circumstances? We discuss this later in this chapter, when we look at how to calculate flexible budgets but a comparison of the differences between fixed and flexible budgets is outlined on page 63 of *The Good Financial Management Guide*.

PREPARING FORECASTS

Voluntary organisations have a variety of income sources, some of which are relatively easy to predict, and others more problematic, for example, a local authority three-year contract compared to a mass appeal to the public. Expenditure can also be easy to calculate but be aware of payments in capital projects such as building works or installing a new computer system which often have 'hidden' problems.

Forecasting is a process that requires asking simple but practical questions such as 'it cost this much last year but how much will it cost next year?' However, more complex information may be required such as intelligence about the organisation's micro and macro environment. For example, the changes in the charity tax regime has seen charities losing income through the withdrawal of Advanced Corporation Tax but potentially gaining income with the flexibility of gift aid without limits. A charity with an investment portfolio would be therefore looking at a decline in income stream whereas an active fundraising charity with supporters who are prepared to gift aid their donations would see an increase.

Internal appraisal of the organisation involves reviewing the current state of an organisation in respect of issues such as its tangible assets, i.e. investments, in relation to intangible assets such as the charity's 'brand' image and position in the market. For example, the charity Guide Dogs for the Blind is very well known. But how high on name recognition is Canine Partners for Independence? Commercial media organisations often undertake market analysis, which can identify public perception broken down by region, age, sex etc of a charity and its position to others. Using a SWOT (strengths, weaknesses, opportunities and threats) analysis of income sources is explained and demonstrated in *The Good Financial Management Guide* (page 64).

Budget preparation also must take into account timing differences between the receipt of income and the payment of expenditure. *The Good Financial Management Guide* provides a useful blank template on how to undertake this process (pages 102-3).

STRUCTURING THE BUDGET

The Good Financial Management Guide (pages 68-82) provides a comprehensive explanation and case study which explains budget headings, reports and implications for cash flow and budgetary control. To summarise:

All budgets – by the time they are issued to managers – are split into lines. Each line is effectively an authorisation to spend or a target to achieve. Budgets also have columns, which split the authorisation into time periods. Additional columns are indented once the budget is operational to allow comparisons to take place between what was expected to happen and what actually happened. The difference between the two is often expressed both in money and percentage terms. These reports may be monthly or sometimes for a management committee quarterly.

In addition a cash flow budget is constructed. The cash budget shows the total expected outflows (payments) and inflows (receipts) during the year. It is vitally important that this budget is prepared so that the organisation is aware of shortages and surpluses during the year. A known cash shortage can be planned for and resolved by, for example, arranging an overdraft. It would be wrong to assume that, if the organisation is in surplus, it does not have a problem. Idle cash means that the opportunity to earn interest is lost. For example, surplus cash of £250,000 over a one-year period could have the following losses and potential earnings with inflation at 2.5 per cent:

		Gross return	after inflation
In a normal current account	=	£0	(£6,250)
In an interest-paying current account at 1%	=	£2,500	(£3,750)
In a deposit account flow to a current account at 4%	=	£10,000	£3,750
On a money market account at 6%	=	£15,000	£8,750

It should also be noted that surpluses shown on a budget or accounts statement and cash surpluses are not the same for a number of reasons:

a. Cash may be paid for the purchase of fixed assets, but the charge in the Income and Expenditure Account (for charities, the Statement of Financial Activities) is depreciation, which is only part of the asset's costs.

b. When a fixed asset is sold there is a profit or loss on sale equal to the difference between the sale proceeds and the 'net book value' of the asset in the balance sheet at the time it is sold. For example, if an asset originally cost £50,000 and depreciation of £35,000 has been charged since its purchase, its net book value will be £15,000. If it is now sold for £11,000 there will be a loss on disposal of £4,000. This loss would be recorded in the accounts, but the effect of the sale would be to increase the organisation's cash by £11,000.

Example of a cash flow budget:

A local group is taking over an additional service from a local authority from 1 September 2001. The following information is given to the voluntary organisation with the comment: 'With our big grant contract in advance and your investments and donations you are not going to have any cash problems' by the local authority's finance officer. The organisation, however, draws up a cash budget to the following 31 March. At 31 August, the voluntary organisation has £12,200 in its bank account.

The group's master revenue budget for the year to 31 March was £500,000, which was financed by a contract of £200,000 paid quarterly in advance. The organisation has investment in properties generating rent revenues of £300,000 paid in even installments on 21 April, 20 September and 20 January.

Of the £500,000 revenue expenditure, £400,000 is made up of salary costs, which are paid on the 25th of each month evenly over the year. £30,000 is paid out evenly in £10,000 instalments at the beginning of October, January and April and £20,000 is paid out in four instalments of £5,000 quarterly, commencing 1 October. Finally the remaining £50,000 is paid out evenly through the year.

There was some small capital expenditure in May comprising £3,000 for office equipment, £5,600 to a builder and £1,450 to an architect, representing 50 per cent of all the bills. The remainder of their bills are due for the furniture to be paid in October and the architect and builder in November. In addition an interest-free loan £20,000 from a supporter of is due for repayment the following August. The organisation has voluntary donations comprising a payroll giving scheme of £5,000 which comes in evenly over the year every month; covenants of £5,000 received in April; and gift aid of £10,000 in December.

Calculation and presentation of the first six months:

Cash Budget from 1 September to 31 March

Income	Sept	Oct	Nov	Dec	Jan	Feb	Mar
Grant	-	50,000	-	-	50,000	-	-
Rent	100,000	-	-	-	100,000	-	-
Donations	416	416	416	10416	416	416	416
Total Income	100,416	50,416	416	10,416	150,416	416	416

Expenditure *Revenue*							
Salaries +NI	33,333	33,333	33,333	33,333	33,333	33,333	33,333
Monthly outgoings	4,166	4,166	4,166	4,166	4,166	4,166	4,166
Other revenue expenditure							
a)	-	10,000	-	-	10,000	-	-
b)	-	5,000	-	-	5,000	-	-
Total Revenue	37,499	52,499	37,499	37,499	52,499	37,499	37,499

Capital							
Furniture	-	3,000	-	-	-	-	-
Builder	-	-	5,600	-	-	-	-
Architect	-	-	1,450	-	-	-	-
Total Capital **Expenditure**	-	3,000	7,050	-	-	-	-

Total Expenditure	37,499	55,499	44,549	37,499	52,499	37,499	37,499
Net Inflow(outflow)	62,917	(5,083)	(44,133)	(27,083)	97,917	(37,083)	(37,083)
Opening Balance (b/forward)	12,200	75,117	70,034	25,901	(1,182)	96,735	59,652
Closing Balance (c/forward)	75,117	70,034	25,901	(1,182)	96,735	59,652	22,569

As you can see, the organisation runs into a minor problem in December, despite the earlier comment! You may very well decide to re-adjust your expenditure plans or alternatively place the surplus funds in September/October and February/March to earn interest, which would pay the charges for the small overdraft facility required.

PROBLEM 3.1

Now attempt a cash budget for the next six months, starting 1 April. Assume a 5 per cent increase in both income and expenditure, except the donations, which are the same.

ANSWER TO PROBLEM 3.1:

Cash Budget from 1 September to 31 March

Income	April	May	June	July	Aug	Sept
Grant	52,500	-	-	52,500	-	-
Rent	105,000	-	-	-	-	105,000
Donations	5,416	416	416	416	416	416
Total Income	**162,916**	**416**	**416**	**52,916**	**416**	**105,416**

Expenditure						
Revenue						
Salaries +NI	35,000	35,000	35,000	35,000	35,000	35,000
Monthly outgoings	4,374	4,374	4,374	4,374	4,374	4,374
Other revenue expenditure						
a)	10,500	-	-	-	-	-
b)	5,250	-	-	5,250	-	-
Total Revenue	**55,124**	**39,374**	**39,374**	**44,624**	**39,374**	**39,374**

Capital						
Loan repayment	-	-	-	-	20,000	-
Total Expenditure	**55,124**	**39,374**	**39,374**	**44,624**	**59,374**	**39,374**

Net Inflow(outflow)	107,792	(38,958)	(38,958)	8,292	(58,958)	66,042
Opening Balance (b/forward)	22,569	130,361	91,403	52,445	60,737	1,779
Closing Balance (c/forward)	130,361	91,403	52,445	60,737	1,779	67,821

Comment

Note that you almost have liquidity problems in August. It is also a good idea to regard cash budgets as a monthly activity, not a yearly task.

Budgets and budgetary control

Budgetary control is the practice of establishing budgets, which identify areas of responsibility. An individual manager is responsible for this budget (e.g. appeals director) and it is the responsibility of the finance department to provide a timely report of comparing actual results against budget from which the manager responsible can either take corrective action or have reassurance that everything is going to plan.

The most important aspect of budgetary control is variance analysis which involves the comparison of actual results during a common period (for operational managers usually a month and for trustees quarterly) with budgeted expectations. The difference between actual results and expected results are called variances.

Small variances are obviously to be expected and do not require special comment – indeed to avoid overwhelming managers with unnecessary information it may be appropriate to provide exception reports, that is, reports which show only large variances. Variances need investigation to determine their cause and to decide what action might be taken to get the organisation back to the plan. One important distinction to make is whether the variance is:

Controllable – in other words, due to factors within the organisation which can be rectified by the management, or

Non-controllable – due to factors outside the control of the organisation. Large non-controllable variances may require a re-think of the plan.

EXAMPLE

A hospice's expenditure on drug supplies for month three is £32,000 against a budget of £28,000. Possible reasons for this might include:

1. Price increases by usual supplier – may be controllable. The person responsible for purchasing should try alternative, more competitive suppliers.

2. Unexpected world prices rise for all aspirin-related drugs – non-controllable. The drug budget may need revising for remainder of year.

3. Spoilage of supplies due to inadequate storage conditions – controllable. Storage problem needs resolving but this may require additional expenditure.

4. Use of expensive branded drugs instead of cheaper alternatives – may be controllable. The hospice needs to look at its purchasing policy.

Note that although budget holders may be required to account for why the variance has occurred, it is not necessarily their actions which have caused it. The point of the control process is to facilitate appropriate action, not to find someone to blame.

The wrong approach to budgetary control is to compare actual results with a fixed budget. As we discussed earlier a fixed budget does not mean that the budget is kept unchanged. Revisions, if required, are made. Instead it means that the budget has been prepared on 'one' estimate of income and expenditure at one level of activity. For example, a homeless night shelter will have 100 rough sleepers, or a cultural centre will have 300 visitors per day in the summer months. No plans are made which show the resulting effect on income and expenditure if the numbers are higher or lower than this. For control purposes you can imagine the problem if the numbers are 20 per cent higher or lower than this.

A flexible control budget recognises both the existence of these problems and the different behaviour of fixed and variable costs. It therefore allows you to relate your input to your output levels for a matching activity in the same period. To enable comparison to be made with the plan it is a good idea to also show the original budget.

EXAMPLE

An advice service may decide on a day case load ratio of one advisor to 20 clients. The assumption is that 60 people will use the centre on any one day and therefore three staff are required. The budget makes this assumption; however, experience shows that actual numbers may be less. The organisation should then prepare a contingency plan for the breakeven point at which it would keep three advisors. Below that figure, say 48, you would only have two advisors. So the client/advisor ratio would increase to 24:1.

The advantage of flexible budget planning is that you can identify problems in advance and have an action strategy available if they do arise. In this case you could have planned alternatives for spare capacity of advisors – for example, researching and writing booklets or have flexible conditions of service for the third advisor.

BUDGETARY CONTROL FIXED V FLEXIBLE

SAMPLE EXERCISE

A disabled person's charity has a trading subsidiary, which is a wood workshop, which makes children's rocking horses for local authority children and foster homes at a set price. Budgeted results and actual results are shown for May 2000.

	Budget	Actual results	Variance
Rocking horses made	100	150	50
	£	£	£
Income (a)	10,000	15,000	5,000
Expenditure:			
Materials	3,000	4,250	(1,250)
Wages	2,000	2,250	(250)
Maintenance	500	700	(200)
Depreciation	1,000	1,100	(100)
Rent and Rates	750	800	(50)
Other Costs	1,800	2,500	(700)
Total Costs (b)	9,050	11,600	(2,550)
Surplus (Deficit) a – b	950	3,400	2,450

Notes

1. In this example, the variances are meaningless for the purposes of control. Costs were higher than budget because there were 50 per cent more rocking horses made. The variable costs would be expected to increase above the budgeted costs. There is no information to show whether control action is required for any aspects of income or expenditure.

2. For control purposes, we need to know:
   a) whether actual costs were higher than they should have been to produce 150 rocking horses
   b) whether actual income was satisfactory from the sale of 150 rocking horses
   c) whether the number of rocking horses made and supplied has varied from the budget in a good or bad way.

The correct approach to budgetary control is to:
1. identify fixed and variable costs
2. produce a flexible budget.

In our example we have the following estimates of cost behaviour:
   a) materials, wages and maintenance costs are variable
   b) rent, rates and depreciation are fixed costs

c) other costs consist of fixed costs of £800 plus a variable cost of £10 per rocking horse made and distributed to the local authorities.

The budgetary control (variance) analysis should be:

	Fixed budget(a)	Flexible budget(b)	Actual (c)	Variance (b) – (c)
Rocking horses made and distributed	100	150	150	
	£	£	£	£
Income	10,000	15,000	15,000	0
Expenditure:				
Variable				
Materials	3,000	4,500	4,250	250
Wages	2,000	3,000	2,250	750
Maintenance	500	750	700	50
Semi-variable costs:				
Other costs	1,800	2,300	2,500	(200)
Fixed Costs				
Depreciation	1,000	1,000	1,100	(100)
Rent and Rates	750	750	800	(50)
Total costs	9,050	12,300	11,600	700
Surplus	950	2,700	3,400	700

> *Discussion:*
>
> 1. *In producing and distributing 150 rocking horses, the expected surplus should be the flexible budget surplus of £2700 rather than the fixed budget surplus of £950. Instead the actual surplus was £3,400, £700 more than expected. The reason for this improvement is that costs are lower than expected as the projected income on 150 horses was exactly as expected.*
>
> 2. *Another reason for the improvement was that the local authorities took all the produced rocking horses. As the cost of producing each unit was less than the price paid by the local authority a surplus (contribution) was made on each rocking horse. What would have happened if the local authority had not taken and paid for the additional rocking horses?*

> 3. **Understanding costs, and in particular the difference between fixed, variable and semi-variable, is vitally important in understanding finance and budgetary control reports (costing is discussed in chapter 5). Issues requiring further investigation are:**
>
> a) **The wages did not rise in exact proportion (controllable variance) and are £750 less.**
> b) **The other variable cost element (controllable variance) is over by £200.**
>
> 4. **The fixed costs are non-controllable and do not require any more attention from the manager's perspective.**

EXERCISE 3.2 – A BUDGETARY CONTROL PROBLEM

St Wilfred's provides a night shelter and day advice centre for the homeless. The budget has been prepared on providing 4,500 free meals every week. Although meals are free, each is recorded with a ticket taken so the organisation can show how many people they are helping. The budget calculations and budgetary control report for Week 17 is being reviewed by the warden and finance officer.

Expenditure	per meal	fixed	variable	total	actual	variance
		£	£	£	£	£
Provisions	50p	0	2,250	2,250	2,200	50
Labour	20p	240	900	1,140	1,180	(40)
Electricity	4p	0	180	180	175	5
Equipment rental	-	500	0	500	500	0
Maintenance	1p	0	45	45	43	2
Management		300	0	300	300	0
		1,040	**3,375**	**4,415**	**4,398**	**17**

The report shows that the organisation is better off by £17. Closer scrutiny of the individual variances shows that labour costs were considerably higher than expected but this has been outweighed by a lower than expected cost for provisions.

As the finance officer, re-work the budget and report your findings if only 4,000 meals were consumed that week.

ANSWER TO EXERCISE 3.2

Expenditure	Per meal	Fixed	Variable	total	actual	Variance
		£	£	£	£	£
Provisions	50p	0	2,000	2,000	2,200	(200)
Labour	20p	240	800	1040	1180	(140)
Electricity	4p	0	160	160	175	(15)
Equipment rental	-	500	0	500	500	0
Maintenance	1p	0	40	40	43	(3)
Management	-	300	0	300	300	0
		1,040	3,000	4,040	4,398	(358)

It now becomes clear that St Wilfred's is actually £358 worse off than it should be at that level of activity. There are no favourable variances and the cost of provisions is actually £200 higher than it should have been for 4000 meals. You must compare like with like to show the true performance.

COMMUNICATING AND COMPUTERISING FINANCIAL INFORMATION

ACTION POINTS FOR YOUR ORGANISATION

Audit your organisation to see if it has:

1. A budget manual

2. A cash budget

3. A flexible budgeting system, particularly for budgetary control reports

4. Appropriate forecasting techniques.

Finance departments and their managers are no longer bookkeepers hidden away in the back of the building surrounded by dusty ledgers. Instead they are responsible for a whole host of duties as outlined in Chapter One and one of the most important of those is communicating financial information for decision-making.

The advent of computerisation in accounting has been one of the major reasons why the finance officer now has such a dynamic role. Previously manual systems would take a long time for everything to be calculated and checked to make sure it balanced. Then from those balances a separate report would then be compiled to produce budget information. Properly set up, a computer system can produce the financial information within days of a month end. Depending on the package, the system design and organisation requirements, a report either produced directly or separately using a spreadsheet can then be supplied to managers.

It is now only the smallest and simplest of organisations which would not benefit from computerising its accounting function and using spreadsheets to model and plan its future. Cash flow projections in particular are perfect for spreadsheet use particularly if the organisation adopts a system of updating the cash flow monthly. *The Good Financial Management Guide* (pages 83-91) covers best practice on communicating financial information, the use of spreadsheets and the stages necessary to computerise an accounting system. To summarise, when communicating financial information it must be:

- Relevant
- Up-to-date
- Accurate
- Intelligible.

WHAT WE HAVE LEARNT

Answer the following questions before checking with the answers in the text.

1. List the key decisions that have to take place in budget planning.

2. Describe the differences between a fixed and flexible budget.

3. What is the purpose of preparing a cash budget?

4. How does variance analysis work?

TEST EXERCISE 3.3

ASH Hospice has devolved a number of service functions into business units and treats them like separate organisations. One unit is 'Medical and Surgery supplies' which supplies products to the Hospice wards. The unit uses the 'just in time method' so no stocks are held, as deliveries from the local hospital are made each day. The unit pays £20 for each pack of raw materials supplied, which it then assembles.

The unit has a budgetary control system, which is based upon fixed budgets, i.e. no adjustment is made for changes in the volume of supplies required. You have recently been appointed as the finance director. You note that actual monthly output is frequently very different from the budgeted output. You are concerned to find that the Hospice Management Team pays little attention to the variances contained in the monthly budgetary report, as they say 'it is now a separate business' and we are only concerned with the 'bottom line'.

The budgetary control report for May 2000 is set out below. You have identified that those items which are marked with V are variable and change directly with output.

You therefore decide to redraft the May 2000 budget report, replacing the original fixed budget with a flexible budget. You also compile a report to the Management Team, which sets out the problems with the original budget format and explains how flexible budgeting could improve the monthly budget report.

Medical Supplies Unit – Original Budget Report for Month of May 2000

Item	Fixed Budget		Actual	Variances
Quantity Supplied (packs)	1,000		1,150	150
	£		£	£
Revenue	100,000	V	120,750	20,750
Costs:				
Supplies	20,000	V	23,000	(3,000)
Wages and Salaries:				
Packing staff	20,000	V	24,150	(4,150)
Maintenance	2,000		1,950	50
Supervision	3,000		2,800	200
Management and administration	4,500		4,650	(150)
	29,500		33,550	(4,050)
Packaging Function:				
Cleaning Equipment	1,000	V	1,035	(35)
Sterilising Equipment	500	V	460	40
Bagging Equipment	250		275	(25)
	1,750		1,770	(20)

Expenses:				
Production	1,250	V	1,495	(245)
Maintenance	1,500		1,550	(50)
Management and Administration	2,300		2,890	(590)
Buildings	850		720	130
	<u>5,900</u>		<u>6,655</u>	<u>(755)</u>

Depreciation:				
Cleaning Equipment	400	V	460	(60)
Sterilising Equipment	1,500	V	1,725	(225)
Bagging Equipment	2,500		2,500	0
Maintenance Equipment	1,300		1,300	0
Office Equipment and Furniture	950		950	0
	<u>6,650</u>		<u>6,935</u>	<u>(285)</u>
Total Costs	<u>63,800</u>		<u>71,910</u>	<u>(8,110)</u>
Surplus (Deficit)	**<u>36,200</u>**		**<u>48,840</u>**	**<u>12,640</u>**

ANSWER TO EXERCISE 3.3

Medical Supplies Unit – Revised budget report for month of May 2000

Item	Flexible Budget	Actual	Variance
Quantity Supplied (packs)	1,150	1,150	0
	£	£	£
Revenue	115,000	120,750	5,750
Variable Costs:			
Supplies	23,000	23,000	0
Packing Staff	23,000	24,150	(1,150)
Cleaning Equipment	1,150	1,035	115
Sterilising Equipment	575	460	115
Production	1,438	1,495	(57)
Depreciation:			
Cleaning Equipment	460	460	0
Sterilising Equipment	1,725	1,725	0
Total Variable Costs	51,348	52,325	(977)
Contribution	63,652	68,425	4,773
Fixed Costs:			
Maintenance Salaries	2,000	1,950	50
Supervision Salaries	3,000	2,800	200
Management & Admin Salaries	4,500	4,650	(150)
Bagging Equipment	250	275	(25)
Maintenance	1,500	1,550	(50)
Management and administration	2,300	2,890	(590)
Buildings	850	720	130
Depreciation:			
Bagging Equipment	2,500	2,500	0
Maintenance Equipment	1,300	1,300	0
Office Equipment & Furniture	950	950	0
Total Fixed Costs	19,150	19,585	(435)
Surplus (Deficit)	44,502	48,840	4,338

MEMORANDUM

To: Management Team

From: Finance Director

Date: 8 June 2000

Reference: Monthly Budgetary Control Reports.

Medical and surgery supplies budgetary control reports compare the actual revenue and costs with a fixed budget, i.e. a budget which does not take into account the effect that changes in output volume have on costs.

This causes two particular problems:

1. The variances for those costs, which are variable, are misleading. For instance, the packing staff wages show an adverse variance of £4,150 for May 2000, but as output was 15 per cent higher than budget there is every likelihood that £3,000 of the variance is simply due to more hours being worked to obtain the higher output.

2. The effect of volume changes on surplus is hidden as variable costs are not grouped together but are included under their particular expense groupings. This means it is difficult to identify the contribution made, or lost, by increases or decreases in the number of supplies made.

The solution to these two problems is to adopt a marginal costing format and flexible budgeting.

A marginal costing format will group the variable costs together and subtract them from the revenue to obtain the contribution for the month. The fixed costs can then be subtracted from the contribution to obtain the surplus. This approach will clearly identify the costs which can be controlled by the medical supplies manager, i.e. the variable costs such as the packing staff wages and those which cannot be changed in the short term, i.e. the fixed costs such as management salaries. This should mean that the manager can concentrate upon the costs they can do something about, rather than being distracted by unavoidable fixed costs.

A flexible budget will adjust the budget for revenue, variable costs and the contribution to take into account the volume of output. As a consequence, the variances which are shown on the budget report will be due to price or efficiency deviations and not caused by volume. This will mean that the manager will be able to concentrate upon dealing with inefficiencies, as the costs of these will be highlighted, instead of being masked by volume changes. For instance, the £3,000 adverse variance for supplies will disappear but there will still be a £1,150 adverse variance on packing staff wages to explain.

Chapter 4
resource management

> **Objectives: By the end of this chapter you should understand:**
> 1. How to maximise resources
> 2. Cash flow planning
> 3. Investment objectives
> 4. Restricted Fund problems
> 5. Overhead cost issues
> 6. Reserves policies.

INTRODUCTION

The theory of public company finance is based on the assumption that the objective of management is to maximise the market value of the company. Voluntary organisations do not share this aim but it is vital that they optimise their use of resources to ensure the organisation is delivering as effectively as possible. For the finance manager this means focusing on the following objectives:

1. Smoothly financing current operations by making the most efficient use of current or liquid funds

2. Maximising available and obtainable resources by enhancing the total return on the invested resources

3. Economising on the use of resources (reducing waste)

4. Channelling resources to facilitate priority activities.

But before you can optimise them the question that needs to be answered is: 'Where do voluntary organisations get their resources from?' *The Good Financial Management Guide* (page 112) reproduces the definitions and sources of finance undertaken for the *UK Voluntary Sector Almanac*, which provides comprehensive statistics on the income and expenditure of the voluntary sector.

How to obtain funds is outside the remit of this manual. Instead we are concerned with optimising the use of these resources. Before examining the various financial techniques to aid optimisation we shall look at the various strategic options which voluntary organisations can consider.

MAXIMISING RESOURCES – STRATEGIC OPTIONS

1. Forming Alliances

Strategic alliances between voluntary organisations can be formed for a variety of reasons and take many different forms. The reasons for such alliances are also sometimes not financial. Alliance forms can include:

a. Consortium arrangements where a group of charities band together to have greater purchasing power

b. Agency arrangements where one charity appoints another to carry out operations on its behalf

c. Joint ventures which as well as being between two charities can also be between a commercial and a voluntary organisation – for example, financial services.

d. Mutual support where charities share information or lobby together.

2. Mergers

Mergers are common in the commercial sector but have until recently been less so in the voluntary sector. A merger is the joining of two organisations to form one organisation. Mergers between voluntary organisations can lead to the generation of significant cost savings and those voluntary organisations are not wasting resources by competing with each other for funding. *The Good Financial Management Guide* (pages 114-5) lists the factors which can lead to a successful merger and those that do not.

3. Outsourcing

Outsourcing is the purchasing of services from third parties that were previously undertaken within the organisation. Virtually anything can be outsourced – from financial services to campaigning activity. Outsourcing is always worth considering if an external provider can safely and reliably perform that activity for less cost or to a higher standard. *The Good Financial Management Guide (*page 116) outlines the benefits of outsourcing and also the problems.

CASH FLOW PLANNING

1. It is essential for the survival of any organisation to have an adequate inflow of cash. A cash flow statement is designed to show where the organisation's cash came from during the year and what it did with it. The statement brings together elements of the balance sheet and the statement of financial activities. A cash flow statement can be a historical statement

or a forecast. It shows the sources and uses of cash over a period of time, whereas the cash budgets we looked at in Chapter 3 shows expected sources and uses of cash weekly or monthly to help in the management of working capital.

The aim of a cash flow statement is to assist the users of accounts to:

1. Assess the organisation's ability to generate positive net cash flows in the future when used as a forecast

2. Assess the organisation's ability to meet its obligations to service loans, pay commitments etc

3. Assess the reasons for differences between reported surplus (deficit) and related cash flows

4. Assess the effect on the organisation's finances of major transactions in the year.

THE CASH FLOW STATEMENT

SAMPLE EXERCISE

New Encounters is a new parents' voluntary organisation, which hopes to provide day support care for autistic children. The parents will run the service themselves supported by session professional staff and helpers.
The organisation began on the 1 January 2001 with an interest-only payable loan from the health and local authority of £51,000 at a preferential rate of 5 per cent, and an endowment loan of £35,000 from one of the parents. The parent say they are not interested in repayment or any interest and the loan need only to be paid back if the organisation were to close. New Encounters purchased fixed assets for £81,000 cash and during the year to 31 December 2001 entered into the following transactions:

1. The service of a fundraising consultancy for £19,500 of which £2,550 was unpaid at the year-end

2. Payments to staff and helpers £10,500 of which £750 was unpaid at the year-end to Inland Revenue

3. Interest on the loan of £2,550 was fully paid in the year

4. Income from charity trusts, fees and activities were £29,400 including £900 debtors at the year-end

5. Interest on cash deposit at the bank amounted to £75.

As the newly appointed honorary treasurer, prepare a historical cash flow statement for the year ended 31 December and comment on the organisation's financial strategy.

Example answer:

New Encounters
Statement of Cash Flows
The Year Ended 31 December 2000

Operating Activities	£	£
Income (29,400-900)	28,500	
Payment to Fundraisers (19,500 – 2,550)	(16,950)	
Payments to Staff (10,500 – 750)	(9,750)	
Cash Flow from Operating Activities		1,800
Returns on Investment and Servicing of Finance:		
Interest Paid	(2,550)	
Interest Received	75	(2,475)
Investing Activities		
Purchase of Fixed Assets	(81,000)	(81,000)
Cash Flow from Investing Activities:		
Endowment	35,000	
Local and Health Authority Loan	51,000	
Cash Flow from Financing Activities		86,000
Net Increase in Cash and Cash Equivalents		4,325
Cash and Cash Equivalents at 1 January 2000		-
Cash and Cash Equivalents at 31 December 2000		4,325

Discussion:

1. The approach of New Encounters to their financing is very similar to the way a commercial organisation would set itself up. Is this appropriate? Instead should not New Encounters:

a) Seek to make the loan from the health and local authority into a grant. The parents are taking some of the responsibility away from the statutory authorities. If it has to be a loan, could New Encounters get a better deal, i.e. interest free with a charge on the fixed assets?

b) The organisation is only showing a surplus in cash due to the loans. Real cash income is only £1,800. The fundraisers have cost £19,500 for an income of only £29,500, a fundraising ratio of 1.5:1 How much have they raised of this income. Are other sources of income raised direct by the charity? The figures need to be broken down.

After reviewing these figures with the committee the treasurer then says: 'I have also prepared for next year a projected cash flow statement. I do have some concerns about our financing strategy.'

The estimates the treasurer used to compile a forecast cash flow statement are outlined. Before looking at the answer, attempt a projected cash flow statement for New Encounters.

1. *A new computer system for £10,300 following the failure of the initial system and the IT company who installed it going insolvent*

2. *Renewal of fundraising consultancy at £18,750 (a reduction of £750 as initial data base costs have been paid). £4,125 will be owed at year-end*

3. *Payments to staff and helpers of £11,250. £600 will be owed at year-end to Inland Revenue*

4. *Loan interest £2,550*

5. *Income from charitable donations etc will be £36,000 (£450 debtors at year-end)*

6. *Interest on bank deposit will be £150.*

EXERCISE ANSWER

New Encounters
Statement of Projected Cash Flows
To the Year ended 31 December 2000

	£	£
Operating Activities		
Income (£36,000 + £900 – £450)	36,450	
Payment to Fundraisers (£18,750 + £2,550 – £4,125)	(17,175)	
Payment to staff (£11,250 + £750 – £600)	(11,400)	
Net Cash Flow from Operating Activities		7,875
Returns on Investment and Servicing of Finance:		
Interest Paid	(2,550)	
Interest Received	150	(2,400)
Investing Activities		
Purchase of Fixed Asset		(10,300)
Cash Flow from Investing Activities:		
Financing Activities		-
Forecast Net Decrease in Cash and Cash Equivalents at 31 December 2001		(4,825)
Cash and Cash Equivalents at 31 December 2001	4,325	
Forecast Cash and Cash Equivalents as at 31 December 2001	(500)	

Discussion

1. The organisation is heading for major financial problems due to:
   a) its initial financial strategy of loans requiring interest repayments and not having sufficient long-term finance to pay for all the fixed assets

   b) insufficient incomes flow to service capital expenditure and then deal with the problem in (c) below

   c) the computer problem.

The computer problem is a 'one off problem' but indicates that, unless an organisation has sufficient liquidity, solvency problems can arise which can threaten the organisation's very existence. The problems are not insurmountable and now the trustees of New Encounters are aware they can take action to rectify the problem. This could include:
   1. Renegotiating loan and interest payment
   2. Reviewing fundraising consultancy performance as previously discussed.

However, the ratio performance has now improved to 1.92:1

THE IMPORTANCE OF PLANNING

The example of New Encounters illustrated how a voluntary organisation must have cash in reserve for unforeseen circumstances. It also highlighted that new organisations in particular need to both have a business plan and budget for revenue surpluses in their early years until a sufficient level of cash is attained. As *The Good Financial Management Guide* (page 125) states:

> '... *the financially prudent organisation plans from the very start to build working capital reserves equivalent to several months' operating expenses*'.

Financial objectives will not be achieved unless the trustees and management know what they are trying to achieve and plan how to achieve those objectives. Quantified financial targets for the achievement of financial objectives should therefore be set out in a financial plan. The financial plan should cover a number of years – three, five, ten years or even longer. The financial plan should be a part of the overall strategic plan of the organisation.

With good financial planning a voluntary organisation can assess in advance its:

a. Short-term cash flow needs
b. Long-term finance needs.

Answering these questions for the plan will mean the organisation will focus on understanding:

1. The management of its cash flow cycle – for example, the management of its debtors and creditors

2. Whether it is likely to have surplus cash and what can be best done with the surplus cash when it arises; alternatively if there is a cash shortage the need to borrow funds and make a 'business case' for them

3. Its income flows and whether it is possible to create reserves from them, e.g. many government sources of finance will only allow a voluntary organisation to 'break even'

4. A reserves policy and target

5. An investment strategy if funds are surplus to need and immediate cash requirements

6. A loan strategy if the organisation is seeking to make long-term asset additions.

Prudent Investment Planning

Once cash assets are accumulated beyond operational needs, consideration can be given to developing permanent investment plans. Statistics on the rate of return between funds left invested short term and funds invested long-term since the 1960s have shown that – except for two small time periods – long-term investments such as company shares (equities) will always outperform short-term investments, i.e. money left in bank money market accounts.

Trustees have a duty to maximise the value of assets and to obtain the best rate of return. However they must not risk investing in highly speculative investments. Equally trustees must also balance the future needs of their charity against current needs. Charities need to decide how much to spend on current beneficiaries as opposed to future requirements.

According to Harrison (1994), there are four key parameters of investment policy, which should be recognised in any statement of investment objectives:

- time horizon
- income needs
- legal powers
- non-financial criteria (i.e. ethical concerns).

Time horizon

As well as providing a dependable source of income, investments also provide a safety net for hard times. The issue for the charity is deciding how quickly the investment would be needed – how liquid it is. This is important because research on long-term investments have shown that they are linked to economic cycles. To really benefit you have to retain the investment through at least one cycle – normally a minimum of three and more likely five years.

Income needs

Investment is a trade-off between immediate income and longer-term capital growth. The more income that is required, the less likely it is that the investment will grow.

Legal powers

The governing documents of the organisation will determine the investment powers of the organisation, for example, what percentage of funds may be invested in company shares, government bonds or cash. The Trustee Act 2000 gives trustees absolute powers of investment but also imposes a general duty on trustees to strike a balance between revenue and capital returns. This is in recognition of the responsibilities that charities have to both current and future beneficiaries.

Non-financial criteria

Charities may wish to exclude investing in certain activities due to them being in conflict with the charity purpose; for example, alcohol rehabilitation charities and the brewing industry. This is a very complex area involving case law, and trustees should always seek professional advice if placing limitations on where they invest. Trustees have to be aware that they must suspend their own personal preferences and act in the best interests of the charity and its beneficiaries. Investment management is a complex area for charities and they should always seek proper advice. In doing so they should always appoint investment advisors by competitive tender. Trustees should also regularly monitor the chosen investment manager's performance against the objectives set. There are various agencies that provide independent assessment of investment performance to assist charities.

RESTRICTED FUNDING AND OVERHEAD COSTS

Most charities have at some time received funds that were subject to restrictions on how they can be spent. Traditionally these funds came from charitable trusts or were donations where the donor imposed conditions. In recent years such restricted funding has also come from statutory sources. Restricted funding means that the voluntary organisation is required by law to separately account for the money. This can be described as making sure that the accounting system can track such funds and prove the money has been spent on the purpose it has been given for. But the problem of restricted funds goes beyond financial accounting and auditing issues. Two major issues arise:

1. At a strategic level the amount of restricted funds can mean that a voluntary organisation can find that its room for manoeuvre or independence is limited if restricted funds are much greater than its general funds which it has discretion to use.

2. Voluntary organisations must take great care in pricing a contract to make sure that all their costs are covered, otherwise they risk subsidising statutory services with charity funds.

Voluntary organisations are not, however, powerless in this process. On appeals to the public careful wording can mean that restrictions are not imposed. If an appeal was restricted, e.g. for a capital project and excess funds were raised, the Charity Commission can give permission to divert the excess funds to similar work undertaken by the charity.

For government contracts, the answer is to carefully cost and in particular make sure that projects cover or make a contribution to overheads. Sometimes funders object to overhead costs because they believe they have nothing to do with the particular activity they are funding. This is wrong: all organisations have overhead costs that are real administration costs and must be paid for. Many funders are resistant to paying overhead costs. *The Good Financial Management Guide* (page 130) outlines three different scenarios and the strategy to overcome them.

FUNDS AND RESERVES

There are various funds a charity can hold. These include:

- **Unrestricted funds** – those funds which are held by the charity with no restriction placed on the use of those funds other than to be within the objects of the charity

- **Designated funds** – these are funds that the charity has designated for a specific project, for example, a building fund. They can be undesignated by the charity if the purpose for which the funds are reserved is not required, as the funds are unrestricted

- **Restricted funds** – these are funds where the donor, or the terms of the appeal, has placed some restrictions on the use of these funds

- **Endowment funds** – these can be permanent or expendable and for a special purpose or general purpose. Often the charity can use the income generated from such funds but is unable to touch the fund itself.

The importance of having the right level of reserves cannot be overstated:

'The required reserve level is the basic building on which all other strategic plan assumptions are built.' (ref: Hind 1995 page 158 – see references page 111)

Official guidance on reserves is now available from the Charity Commission (CC19). The Charity Commission defines reserves as income that becomes available to the charity and is to be expended at the trustees' discretion in furtherance of any of the charity's objectives (sometimes referred to as 'general-purpose income'), but which is not yet spent, committed or designated (i.e. is 'free'). This excludes the following (as defined by CC19):

ACTION POINTS FOR YOUR ORGANISATION

Review to see if you have:

1. Arrangements with other organisations

2. Outsourced any activities

3. Prepared forecast cash flow statements

4. A financial plan, which shows how cash balances are created or what it does with excess cash balances

5. Recently reviewed the organisation's investment manager

6. An accounting system that can track restricted funds

7. Fundraisers who are aware of how to word appeals so as not to create restricted funds

8. A policy on how to apportion overhead costs

9. A reserves policy.

- Permanent endowments
- Expendable endowments
- Restricted funds
- Designated funds for proper purposes
- Income funds that could only be realised by disposing of fixed assets properly held for charity use.

Charities are now required in their Annual Reports to explain and justify the level of reserves. A statement outlining the reserves policy of the organisation usually meets this. The policy should cover:

1. The reason why the charity needs reserves

2. The level or range of reserves the trustees believe the charity needs

3. What steps the charity is going to take to establish or maintain the reserves at the agreed level (or range)

4. Arrangements for monitoring and reviewing the policy.

The Good Financial Management Guide provides two flow charts demonstrating how to develop a reserves policy and the place of the reserves policy in the planning process (pages 133 and 134). Reserves policies should be kept under constant review and require input at the highest level of the organisation. As Hind states:

'In the charity context, it would appear, at first sight, to be a simple exercise to quantify the level of an individual charity's reserves and decide whether it is appropriate in the context of that charity's operations. In practice, it is far from straightforward. It warrants close examination because if charities do not get this right the integrity of their strategic planning process will be undermined.' (Hind 1995 p51)

WHAT HAVE WE LEARNT

Answer the following questions before checking in the text:

1. Describe the various alliances voluntary organisation can form.

2. How is cash flow planning different from a cash budget?

3. What are the aims of a cash flow statement?

4. With good financial planning what will a voluntary organisation understand?

5. What are Harrison's four key parameters of investment policy?

6. Describe the various reserves a charity can hold.

EXERCISE 4.1

SAMPLE EXERCISE

Work through the following:

The new honorary treasurer of Age Concern Winton is reviewing the management accounts prior to the management committee meeting with the finance officer.

Age Concern Winton (ACW) provides the following services:
- A drop-in day centre offering various leisure and educational activities
- A refreshments and lunch-time meal service
- A new home visit service which starts on the first day of the new financial year.

In addition ACW runs two shops selling donated and new 'fair goods'. It receives income from various financial services (insurance) as well as the occasional legacy.

ACW has a director who is supported by the following staff:
- An activities co-ordinator
- A home visits co-ordinator
- A catering manager and supervisor
- Two shop managers
- A finance officer
- A secretary/administrator.

ACW is based in its own building, which was donated to it five years ago. A local estate agent has estimated the building would be worth £150,000 and derives an annual rent of £10,000 per annum.

The building is divided into 40 per cent of the space being for the education and leisure activities, 40 per cent for meals and 20 per cent for offices. Within these offices the home visits co-ordinator is based, who takes up 10 per cent of the space.

An annual budget is prepared each year by the finance officer with help from the honorary treasurer from the latest estimates based on last year's financial accounts. These also form the financial reports provided to the trustees and staff. The first draft budget and the finance officer notes are:

ACW budget for the year

1. Salaries (inclusive of on costs):

	£	£
Director	28,000	
Finance officer	20,000	
Co-ordinators	40,000	
Canteen manager	16,000	
Catering supervisor	12,000	
Shop managers	22,000	
Secretary	16,000	154,000

2. Overheads

Home visit volunteer exps	6,000	
Shop purchases	18,000	
Shop rent and rates	7,000	
Leisure material	3,000	
Cleaning	4,000	
Audit	3,000	
Food purchases	14,000	
Telephone, post and stationery	7,000	
Shop telephones	3,000	
Insurances	5,000	
Shop insurances	4,000	
Travel	6,000	
Sundries	8,000	
Shop cleaning	2,000	
Capital kitchen equipment	5,000	<u>95,000</u>
Total expenditure		<u>249,000</u>

3. Income

	£	£
Funds brought forward		16,500
Central grant from local authority		80,000
Activities services grant		30,000
Activities services charitable grant		10,000
Home visits contract		20,000
Shop sales		60,000
Catering sales		30,000
Home visits		6,000
Legacy		10,000
Financial services		6,000
Total income		<u>269,500</u>
Surplus of income over expenditure		20,500

Notes to the budget

1. A pay rise of 3 per cent for the year has been budgeted. On costs are 10.5 per cent with 3 per cent contribution to a personal pension scheme paid gross.

2. Home visits – volunteer expenses are priced at £3 per visit. Local authority contract is based on a per capita charge of £10 per visit, paid 10 days after receipt of a monthly visit report.

3. The legacy has been confirmed and is due to be paid during the fifth month of the year. It has restrictions and is to be spent only on the education and activities projects.

4. Catering meals are priced at 75p per meal day ticket, comprising morning coffee, lunch and afternoon tea. The price is based on what the catering manager, supported by the users catering committee and the local health authority representatives, considers to be an appropriate price and service for old people needing a good meal. There are 160 places a day available.

5. Funds within the charity comprise:
   Restricted funds of £10,000 for education projects
   General fund, £11,500
   Designated fund for kitchen equipment, £5,000
   Cash at bank, £21,000
   6% capital bond in the local building society maturing in two years' time, purchase value £10,000. The bond pays no income to avoid paying income tax.

6. Grants are paid mid-quarterly.

7. Shop sales are even throughout the year except in months 5 and 12 when they are respectively half and double normal takings, reflecting one shop being closed in month 5 and Christmas in month 12.

8. Purchases are paid monthly in arrears. Current food stocks are valued at £1,200; shop stocks £1,500. New kitchen equipment is to be installed in month 2 and is payable on delivery.

9. Payment for all operational services are paid weekly, except for professional and overhead administrative expenses which are paid quarterly in arrears. There is £5,000 outstanding overhead expenditure at the start of the year.

10. A charitable trust pays a grant of £10,000 for the activity services on the first day after the end of the half-year – in full.

Discussion:

The honorary treasurer is unhappy with the budget, pointing out that activities should be reflected in cost centres and how much each contributes to covering general overheads. Equally, as there is no cash flow forecast. Can the organisation pay its way for the following year?

They are also not happy with the views of the catering manager and believe there should be changes in the planning process in the future for determining the budget for projects/cost centres?

STAGE 1: PREPARE A NEW BUDGET BASED ON COST CENTRES

Answer to Stage 1

Actual Budget

Cost centres/projects	Catering	Shops	Activities	Home visits	Total
	£	£	£	£	£
Sales	30,000	60,000			90,000
Purchases	(14,000)	(18,000)			(32,000)
Gross profit					58,000
Project income			40,000	26,000	66,000
Total income	16,000	42,000	40,000	26,000	124,000
Direct expenditure					
Salaries	28,000	22,000	20,000	20,000	90,000
Rent & rates	4,000	7,000	4,000	200	15,200
Leisure activities			3,000		3,000
Cleaning	1,600		1,600	80	3,280
Shop cleaning		2,000			2,000
Shop telephone		3,000			3,000
Shop insurance		4,000			4,000
Vol. expenses				6,000	6,000
	33,600	38,000	28,600	26,280	126,480
Contribution to general overheads	(17,600)	4,000	11,400	(280)	(2,480)

Expenses, salaries	(64,000)
Cleaning	(720)
Audit	(3,000)
Tel, post & stationery	(7,000)
Insurances	(5,000)
Travel	(6,000)
Sundries	(8,000)
Rent & rates	(1,800)
Sub total	(95,520)
Operating profit (loss)	(98,000)
Central grant	80,000
Legacy	10,000
Financial service	6,000
Rent in kind income	10,000
	106,000
Surplus on budget	8,000

STAGE 2: PREPARE A CASH FLOW BUDGET

Answer to Stage 2

Cash flow

Income	1	2	3	4	5	6	Total
	£	£	£	£	£	£	£
Central grant from local authority		20,000			20,000		40,000
Activities service grant		7,500			7,500		15,000
Activities service fees							0
Home visits contracts		1,666	1,666	1,666	1,666	1,666	8,330
Shop sales	4,800	4,800	4,800	4,800	2,400	4,800	26,400
Catering sales	2,500	2,500	2,500	2,500	2,500	2,500	15,000
Home visits	500	500	500	500	500	500	3,000
Legacy					10,000		10,000
Financial services	500	500	500	500	500	500	3,000
	8,300	37,466	9,966	9,966	45,066	9,966	120,730
Expenditure							
Salaries	12,833	12,833	12,833	12,833	12,833	12,833	76,998
Shop purchases	1,500	1,500	1,500	1,500	1,500	1,500	9,000
Food purchases	1,200	1,167	1,167	1,167	1,167	1,167	7,035
Operational services	3,000	3,000	3,000	3,000	3,000	3,000	18,000
Professional and admin expenses	5,000	-	-	5,500	-	-	10,500
Kitchen equipment	-	5,000	-	-	-	-	5,000
	23,533	23,500	18,500	24,000	18,500	18,500	126,533
Cash inflow/outflow	(15,233)	13,966	(8,534)	(14,034)	26,566	(8,534)	(5,803)
Balance brought f/ward	21,500	6,267	20,233	11,699	(2,335)	24,231	21,500
Balance carried f/ward	6,267	20,233	11,699	(2,335)	24,231	15,697	15,697

STAGE 3 DISCUSS FINDINGS FROM NEW MANAGEMENT ACCOUNTS AND CASH FLOW:

Answer to Stage 3

Interpretation of data

- During month 4 the charity is currently scheduled to go into deficit.
- The charity either needs to plan how it is to deal with the situation, i.e. by raising further funds or by entering into negotiations with the bank to arrange a short-term overdraft.
- The information received in respect of the shops does not give meaningful information as to whether one of the shops is making losses or not – further work would need to be done on the shops.

Taking into account the views of the catering manager:

- At present the people receiving catering meals are being charged 75p for the whole day. This includes morning coffee, lunch and afternoon tea. If coffee and tea were charged separately at 25p each day then this would result in an increased receipt per day of 50p, that is:

    – Coffee   25p
    – Lunch including tea or coffee   75p
    – Tea   25p
    – Making a total of   125p

- Current budget is based on:

    250 days (i.e. 52 weeks x 5 days = 260 days) – 10 days in respect of Christmas and other holidays)

    at total capacity of 160 people which is perhaps unlikely

    More prudent budget is 160 maximum less 25% void = 120

    £1.25 x 250 days x 120 places = £37,500

- Calculate a new cash flow:

ANSWER – NEW CASH FLOW TAKING INTO ACCOUNT REVISED CHARGES

Cash flow 2

Income	1	2	3	4	5	6	Total
	£	£	£	£	£	£	£
Central grant from local authority		20,000			20,000		40,000
Activities service grant		7,500			7,500		15,000
Activities service fees							0
Home visits contracts		1,666	1,666	1,666	1,666	1,666	8,330
Shop sales	4,800	4,800	4,800	4,800	2,400	4,800	26,400
Catering sales	3,125	3,125	3,125	3,125	3,125	3,125	18,750
Home visits	500	500	500	500	500	500	3,000
Legacy					10,000		10,000
Financial services	500	500	500	500	500	500	3,000
	8,925	38,091	10,591	10,591	45,691	10,591	124,480
Expenditure:							
Salaries	12,833	12,833	12,833	12,833	12,833	12,833	76,998
Shop purchases	1,500	1,500	1,500	1,500	1,500	1,500	9,000
Food purchases	1,200	1,167	1,167	1,167	1,167	1,167	7,035
Operational services	3,000	3,000	3,000	3,000	3,000	3,000	18,000
Professional and admin expenses	5,000	-	-	5,500	-	-	10,500
Kitchen equipment	-	5,000	-	-	-	-	5,000
	23,533	23,500	18,500	24,000	18,500	18,500	126,533
Cash inflow/outflow	(14,608)	14,591	(7,909)	(13,409)	27,191	(7,909)	(2,053)
Balance brought f/ward	21,500	6,892	21,483	13,574	165	27,356	19,447
Balance carried f/ward	6,892	21,483	13,574	165	27,356	19,447	17,394

Notes: Reworked for the additional fees due to tea and coffee

New cash flow forecast:
a) Resolves deficit and now moves to surplus.
b) Resolves cash flow problem – £625 extra per month.

i.e. £37,500/12 = £3,125 per month less £2,500 originally received.

Cash position
In respect of the bond of £10,000, the charity pays no income tax. It may be worth considering redeeming the bond and keeping it as a bank deposit in order to smooth the charity through its cashflow problems.

Use of the cash budget
In month four ACW was scheduled to go into deficit and, although plans are implemented to avert this, there is only a surplus of £165. This surplus could easily disappear if something unforeseen happens. The budget could be used to take to the bank manager to discuss an approved overdraft. The bond could be used as security and approved overdrafts carry lower rates of interest than unapproved ones.

Chapter 5
special financial tools

> **Objectives: By the end of this chapter you should understand:**
>
> 1. How to evaluate the performance of your organisation
> 2. How to apply ratio analysis to your own accounts
> 3. Costing a service
> 4. Overhead costs
> 5. Activity-based costing
> 6. Cost behaviour
> 7. Breakeven analysis.

INTRODUCTION

This chapter looks at specialist financial analysis applied to charities and the issues of cost accounting. Increasingly, voluntary organisations are being placed in competitive situations – for example, in winning a contract from a local authority. Registered charities are being more closely examined particularly on their administrative costs and how much they have spent to raise funds. The effective voluntary organisation is one that understands its cost structure and ensures that all its overhead costs are covered. A registered charity now needs to publicly demonstrate that it is financially sound, efficient and economic.

PERFORMANCE MONITORING

In the commercial sector, one helpful approach to accounts analysis is to ask the question: 'Should I invest my money in this company?' Charities are not commercial organisations and do not have profit and loss or an accounts format, which give a bottom line of how much profit has been made. In the absence of normal commercial criteria to analyse accounts, work has now been undertaken to develop measurements of performance especially for charities. Some of the measurements reviewed are the same as for commercial organisations, whereas others are adapted or are unique to charity organisations, for example, liquidity

Many small businesses often go bankrupt even though they are profitable due to problems with cash flow and therefore are unable to pay their bills. Many methods of analysis have been developed to assess commercial liquidity and some of these methods – called ratios – can be applied to charities with one important difference! Cash will have little or no restriction in a commercial organisation, but in a charity it may be restricted. Can we count restricted funds backed by cash as part of our cash available to pay bills?

Aims, Inputs, Outputs and Outcomes

Before exploring techniques for analysing accounts a comment on management information techniques developed in the absence of the profit line, by not-for-profit organisations. Charities have been encouraged to focus on *aims* and objectives. For example, the aim of an age concern organisation may be to provide:

> '*A service for older people which aims to enhance the quality of life by providing a safe, manageable and comfortable environment, social stimulation and companionship, thereby relieving loneliness and providing respite care for carers*'.

Inputs is the term used to denote the resources used in the production of outputs. Inputs for the above services may include staff salaries, costs of activities, refreshments etc. Inputs should be captured by the accounting system and will generally follow an accounting code classification according to the payment. Inputs will also include the income payments to finance the service whether it is a service charge or a grant.

For commercial consideration the respective inputs of income and expenditure would be added up and taken away from each other and either a surplus (profit) or deficit (loss) would be calculated. Internal management accounts drawn up as budgets in this traditional format would be prepared and monitored regularly by the directors.

For a commercial organisation such reports would now be the end of the story and any profit would be distributed to owners. But is this sufficient for charity trustees?

We would argue, emphatically, it is not. The intention of providing a day care service and the role of trustees should be to establish if the aims of the service were achieved. This is not found out from the simple budget against actual financial statement.

To ascertain these answers, the term *outputs* has been used. Outputs cannot always be expressed in financial value terms. In the absence of money values to measure whether the service has been delivered, other methods have to be developed. Ideally these should be quantitative in nature as they allow for a degree of objectivity and can be easily measured and understood and allow for comparison whether it is against an initial target, previous years or another similar service.

For example, a measurable output may be the number of people attending an Age Concern day service. This can be compared against planned numbers and compared over time to see how well the service is used.

Outputs, however, are very different from outcomes. The *outcome* of the day care service mentioned would be to discover the extent to which a person's quality of life improved. This inevitably becomes a value judgement but it is still possible to seek quantitative information using questionnaires and feedback from carers and relatives.

RATIO ANALYSIS

Ratio analysis is used to identify trends, recognise strengths and pinpoint weaknesses that may not be readily apparent. *The Good Financial Management Guide* (page 151) discusses and demonstrates appropriate ratios, which can be used by voluntary organisations. There are three simple stages in undertaking ratio analysis:

1. Put into simple numbers
Reduce the numbers down to a manageable size and then convert them into ratios. Reducing numbers is simply done by rounding down the numbers to three or four significant figures. The next stage is to turn the numbers into ratios. A ratio is a way of showing the size of a number relative to another number. For example, when driving a car it is normal to keep an eye on the ratio of distance/time (that is, miles per hour), in order to judge speed. Similarly, the ratio of distance/fuel used (that is, miles per gallon), which gives us the one observes principal indicator of the efficiency of the car.

2. Compare
The only sensible way of drawing a conclusion about a statistic is to use it to make a comparison. For instance, it is pointless to say that we served 4,000 meals in our day centre unless it can be compared with how many were served in the previous year or the number of meals we planned to serve.

3. Draw your own conclusions
The conclusion arrived at after following this process should be much better than the views at the start. Try and list your views before the process and compare them with your views after you have analysed the accounts.

EXERCISE 5.1

Using your own organisation's accounts, calculate the following ratios:

- Charitable expenditure/total expenditure

- Charitable expenditure/total income

- Administrative expenditure/total expenditure

- Investment income/investment value

- Cost of generating funds/total income

- Cost of generating funds/voluntary income.

> **Cost accounting:**
> Most simply, costs are the financial value(s) of the resources used to develop a service. You need to be clear of the full range of resources which go into a service and their financial value.

EXERCISE 5.2

In costing the provision of a hot lunch service in a day centre, list the factors you would have to take into consideration:

1.

2.

3.

4.

5.

6.

> The answer to the above should have included such items as food, staff wages, electric or gas, rent and rates. Key issues of costing are raised by this example — what are the full range of resources used to provide a service; how much of these resources are devoted to this service alone, and how much is shared among a number of services; and how should their financial value be calculated?

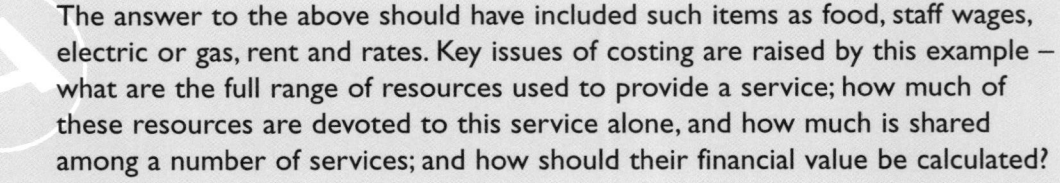

When calculating costs it is useful to do so against two dimensions:

- the type of expenditure
- the site (project) at which the activity occurred – referred to as a 'cost centre', for example, at three sites:

COST CENTRE

	a	b	c
Salaries	£108000	£100,000	£92,000
Travel			
Heat/light			

This is also useful for control purposes as it allows reports comparing the budget against the actual activity to be compiled during the year and at the year-end:

Cost Centre a Month 4	Actual for Period £	Budget for Period £	Variance £	Actual to Date £	Budget to Date £	Variance £	Annual Budget £
Salaries	8,780	9,000	220	35,120	36,000	880	108,000
Travel							
Heat/light							
etc							
Total	—	—	—	—	—	—	—

COSTING A SERVICE

Unit costs are the simplest and most common way to cost a service. This method recognises the cost of one part or 'unit' in a service. Depending upon the nature of the activity it could be a cost per service user, per component or staff member. This is important as it:

- helps gauge the relative efficiency, either of parts of the service compared to other parts or to another organisation;

- helps in the preparation of tenders for contracts and to decide the appropriate fee to charge.

OVERHEAD COSTS

These are costs which are incurred by the organisation as a whole and are usually apportioned to the different cost centres. There is no one method of dividing these costs, but the most simple and common is called absorption costing which is to spread all the cost into the centres.

In separating out overhead costs for absorption, it is useful to think of the total costs at each cost centre as comprising four elements:

1. Direct costs of the service

2. Indirect costs which are incurred in support of the actual service and are usually carried out within – or linked to the service itself – such as heating/lighting of office for the service

3. Overhead costs which are the costs of the headquarters and central services of the organisation – chief executive salary etc

4. Capital related costs – interest repayments or depreciation upon any equipment.

Two alternatives to dealing with overhead costs are:

a. Workload charging. Central services charge a fee for their services directly to other parts of the organisation

b. Service load agreements. A level of service is agreed at a pre-determined price.

Unit Costs and Analysis – a warning

There are limitations to using unit costs to evaluate or compare different services and cost centres. Comparison of costs alone is not sufficient, as other elements can obscure differences:

- the complexity of the needs being met and in the quality of the service being provided;

- the accommodation a service is operating from, which could affect its costs;

- significant regional differences in salaries or costs for a national organisation;

- how different services may be treating their costs.

ACTIVITY-BASED COSTING

Dissatisfaction with traditional costing methods, and in particular the application of overhead costs, led to the development of activity-based costing (ABC) in the 1980s. What makes ABC different is that it takes the perspective that overheads do not just occur and have to be allocated in some formula but instead are real costs caused by activities or cost drivers. Instead of thinking of overheads as rendering a service to units of cost, the dynamic approach of ABC sees overheads being created by cost units. Thus overheads should be charged according to the costs which have caused them. The advantage of ABC is that it replaces the arbitrary nature of overhead apportionment, which can be inefficient and cause conflict with the direct service operations of a voluntary organisation with a more transparent system. Advocates of ABC argue that overhead costs can be analysed and cost drivers identified.

Critics of ABC argue that analysis of overheads to identify the cost drivers is time-consuming and the cost savings associated do not justify it. *The Good Financial Management Guide* (page 163) outlines the specific problems associated with ABC application to the voluntary sector. It concludes that ABC is primarily relevant to very large charities, which could justify the expense involved in having the sophisticated computer systems to provide the information to undertake ABC analysis. However, it further argues that as a one-off analysis exercise ABC can be used by all organisations.

COST BEHAVIOUR

The basic principle of cost behaviour is that as a level of activity rises, so costs will usually rise. The problem is, in what ways do costs rise and by how much, as the level of output increases? Costs can be divided into fixed and variable:

- A fixed cost is one that does not change with outputs: a professional salary; rental of a telephone line

- A variable cost does vary with a level of output: a sessional worker as sessions increase; telephone charges as you make a call

- You can also have costs that are a mixture of the two, for example, a second telephone line. Here your fixed costs increase like a step:

```
                    ┌─────────── line 1 + line 2 New Fixed Cost
────────────────────┘ line 1 Fixed Cost
```

Salaries equally can have a fixed element and then a variable element, i.e. overtime payments. These are called semi-fixed or mixed costs.

EXERCISE 5.3

Reviewing the need for vehicles at its projects three different mileage uses are proposed ranging from 15,000 to 25,000 to 40,000 miles. What are the costs of vehicles at these different rates?

The following information is obtained per vehicle:

1. Vehicle leases are £3,000
2. Petrol and oil cost 10p per mile
3. Tyres cost £400 per set to replace. They require replacement at 25,000 miles
4. Fixed maintenance costs are £175 per annum
5. Tax and insurance are £300 per annum.

Answer

The costs can be divided into fixed, variable and mixed (step) costs.

Fixed costs are:	£ per year
Leasing charge	3,000
Maintenance	175
Tax, insurance	300
	3,475

Variable costs are:

Petrol and oil	10p per mile

Step costs are:

Tyre replacement at 25,000 miles. Therefore at:

15,000 miles	no cost
25,000 miles	£400
40,000 miles	£400

The estimated yearly costs then are:

	15,000	25,000	40,000
	£	£	£
Fixed costs	3,475	3,475	3,475
Variable costs (10p per mile)	1,500	2500	4,000
Step costs	0	400	400
Total	<u>4,975</u>	<u>6,375</u>	<u>7,875</u>

BREAK-EVEN ANALYSIS

In calculating a budget your income and expenditure may be exactly equal, that is you 'break-even'. A voluntary organisation tendering for a local government contract may wish this. In reality the actual accounts will probably be a small surplus or deficit but in tendering for the contract you wish to ensure that you are not going to make a loss or at least determine what losses could happen. Break-even analysis is used to assess whether a particular activity should be undertaken.

To use break-even analysis you must understand the concept of contribution. This is calculating how much of your variable income less expenditure is required to cover your fixed costs.

EXAMPLE:

SAMPLE EXERCISE

A voluntary drug counselling service is financed by fees of £500 for every client seen. The organisation has certain fixed costs. In preparing the budget, it would be useful to know at what point does the variable income less variable expenditure cover the fixed costs.

The costs are as follows:

Annual fixed costs	£462,500.00
Variable cost per client	£17.50

Calculation:
Contribution per client £500 – £17,50 =	£482.50
Breakeven point = £462,500/£482.50 =	958 clients

The project requires 958 clients to break even, in other words to cover its fixed costs.

To calculate the break-even point you need first to work out the contribution per unit. This is done by taking the variable costs away from the variable income per unit. If total fixed costs are then divided by this contribution per unit, the number of units needed to break-even will be found.

EXERCISE 5.4

The chief executive of a local benefits advice centre has been approached by a commercial organisation to sponsor a briefing pack on advice services.

The company has said that rather than give a fixed donation it will instead give the organisation £20 for each pack that is sold up to 5,000 packs. Costs of producing the pack have to be met up-front by the advice centre. The trustees meet to consider the offer and the chief executive who has suggested selling the pack for £21, provides the following figures:

Fixed cost of producing packs	£42,500	
Variable cost per pack	£5.50	
Income per pack	£21.00	
Profit per pack	£15.50	
	× 5000 =	£77,500
Profit on venture		£35,000

The honorary treasurer says they are unhappy with the figures.

Why?

What further information would be useful in making a decision?

76 SPECIAL FINANCIAL TOOLS

ANSWERS TO EXERCISE

Exercise 5.4

There may be some ethical issues over whether an advice centre should be involved with a commercial company. Assuming these issues can be overcome what else is wrong?

The organisation has not undertaken any external analysis. In particular would the organisation be able to 'sell' 5,000 packs? What would happen if it did not? One task to support the external appraisal would be to ascertain the number of packs that need to be sold in order to at least break-even.

Contribution per pack – selling price £21 - £5.50 (variable cost) = £15.50

Break-even point = £42,500/£15.50 = 2,742.

Can the organisation 'sell' 2,742 packs? Remember despite the sponsorship, the organisation still has the up-front cost of producing them.

> **Audit your organisation by checking to see:**
>
> 1. Whether the trustees receive ratio analysis reports
>
> 2. Whether the organisation understands its costs!
>
> 3. What method of apportioning overheads has been used
>
> 4. Whether ABC can be applied to your organisation
>
> 5. Whether projects are appraised using break-even analysis.
>
> *ACTION POINTS FOR YOUR ORGANISATION*

Break-even analysis is a powerful decision-making tool but, as *The Good Financial Management Guide* (p169) outlines, it does have limitations.

WHAT HAVE WE LEARNT

Attempt to answer these questions before checking the text:

1. What is the difference between outputs and outcomes?

2. Can ABC costing techniques be applied to voluntary organisations?

3. Describe cost behaviour.

EXERCISE 5.5

The Captain Nelson Foundation has a residential services department, which runs three residential centres for disabled, elderly, former sailors. The details are:

Name of home	Number of beds	Beds occupied	Staff establishment
Southways	40	30	8
Northend	40	20	8
Central	50	40	10

Health and local authorities pay the Nelson £3,500 per annum per resident in occupation. Variable overheads are £500 per annum per occupied bed. Fixed costs are staff whose average salary is £10,000 per annum each, and charity head office overheads at £200 per bed.

At a management team meeting reviewing the homes, the finance director states that the homes are currently running at a deficit. The charity can no longer afford these deficits and so he informs the residential homes director that a revised budget is required which will, at a minimum, break even.

At a subsequent meeting of the heads of the homes to discuss options, the Central home head suggests that Northend be closed and the residents transferred to the other homes. The residential services director points out that two staff are shortly to leave. By reducing the establishment at Northend to six, it is suggested that this should resolve the problem.

Questions

1. Calculate the current residential homes department deficit by home.

2. What is the required number to break even?

3. Adopting the suggestion to lose two members of staff at Northend, what is the new position for the department? Assume the same occupancy but 10 per cent rise in income and costs.

4. Discuss the advantages/disadvantages of the proposed solution. Are there alternatives?

EXERCISE 5.6

Understanding overhead costs in tendering to run a day centre

Following re-organisation, Any Council now comprises two main urban areas at either end of its boundary separated by countryside. One of the urban areas is the county town and has an active and large Age Concern organisation – ACCT. In the other smaller urban town the services are still provided by the Council. The new Council has asked ACCT if it would like to run the same services in the urban town. It currently gives a grant of £80,000 to ACCT and it is proposed to offer a further grant of £45,000 to run the urban town's services. The Council will transfer its current building rent free to ACCT. There are no transfers or contractual problems for the existing staff as the Council will re-deploy existing staff if ACCT takes over.

The current ACCT Organisation has a large purpose-built building owned by the organisation, which accommodates 150 people daily in a variety of activities, advice, medical, etc services. The building has an average 80 per cent capacity use. The Urban town centre is half the size of the county town centre with 75 places and exactly half the running costs. The budget of ACCT for the current year is:

Income:	£
Council grant	80,000
Insurance/services	16,000
Donations	17,000
Catering profit	13,500
Total	126,500
Expenditure:	
Staff	104,000
Costs	22,000
Total	126,000
Surplus	500

The director has made the following notes on the budget with a plan for the take-over of the new service. They have proposed that both centres will be under their overall management assisted by the finance officer and catering manager all of whom would accept a 10 per cent pay rise to reflect additional responsibilities and time for managing both services (all staff costs are inclusive of NI etc):

1. A director £25,000 – who has advised that the urban town centre will need a centre manager at £22,000

2. A secretary £15,000 – who has estimated that admin costs at the other centre will be £7,500

3. A finance officer £20,000 – who has advised that the urban centre will require a finance assistant at £10,000

4. Service co-ordinators (both part-time at £10,000 each)

5. A catering manager £12,000 – who has advised they would need an assistant at the urban town centre at £10,000

6. Service session staff £12,000; volunteers' expenses £4,000

7. Building running costs £10,000. The new centre will be half in size

8. Office, admin audit £8,000. Admin costs at the urban centre will be £2,000

9. Lunchtime meals are charged at £1.00 and two tea/coffee sessions at 25p per session. A profit of 30 per cent is made on catering. The centre and catering services are open for 250 days a year

10. Donations and service income for the new centre will be equal in proportion to current ACCT

Questions

From the perspective of ACCT would you take the Council's offer and take over the new service?

The proposed new management arrangements would mean moving from being one organisation on one site to being an organisation with a management team managing two sites. Prepare revised budgets for the new organisation.

ANSWER TO EXERCISES

Exercise 5.5

1.

	Southways	Northend	Central	Total
	£	£	£	£
Income per bed	3,500	3,500	3,500	
Less variable overheads	500	500	500	
	3,000	3,000	3,000	
Occupied beds	30	20	40	90
Total Income	90,000	60,000	120,000	270,000
Fixed costs				
Overheads (£200 x beds)	8,000	8,000	10,000	26,000
Staff (£10000 x numbers)	80,000	80,000	100,000	260,000
Total Expenditure	88,000	88,000	110,000	286,000
Surplus (Deficit)	**2,000**	**(28,000)**	**1,0000**	**(16,000)**

Deficit for the department as a whole £16,000

2.

Break-even:	88,000/3,000	88,000/3,000	110,000/3,000
	= 29.3	= 29.3	= 36.6

3.

	Southways	Northend	Central	Total
Income	3,850	3,850	3,850	
Less overheads	550	550	550	
	3,300 x30	3,300 x20	3,300 x40	
Total Income	99,000	66,000	132,000	297,000
Less:				
Overheads	8,800	8,800	11,000	28,600
Staff	88,000	66,000	110,000	264,000
	96,800	74,800	121,000	292,600
Surplus (Deficit)	**2,200**	**(8,800)**	**11,000**	**4,400**

Revised budget now gives the department a £4,400 surplus.

4. Issues for discussion

a) Staff losses do not resolve deficit and could they manage with less than the number of staff re : rotas, commitments and health and safety?

b) Closing the third home would give an even greater surplus but what would be the social and disruption costs to the residents?

c) Could the homes seek other residents from similar charities to increase occupancy?

d) A detailed plan looking at the charity's responsibilities and needs should be prepared before any decision is made.

Exercise 5.6 – version 1

The new organisation will be offering 225 persons facility, 150 places in the county town and 75 places in the urban town.

There are management implications. On the assumption that the service will be jointly managed but also require additional staff there is the issue of overheads. Current management costs are:

	£
Director	25,000
Finance	20,000
Catering	12,000
Total	57,000

Assuming the trustees agree the director's, finance and catering managers' 10 per cent increase: current total salaries of £57,000 x 10% = £5,700. Revised management costs are £62,700. This could be allocated on service level criteria of 225 places. Therefore 62,700/225 = £278.66 x 75 places = £20,899.

Trading Income from catering at current 80% usage –
Coffee   25p
Tea   25p
Lunch   100p
Total £1.50 per day x 60 persons (80% of 75) x 250 days = £22,500 x 30% = £6,750.

An initial Income and Expenditure Budget for the urban town centre can now be drawn up:

Income:
Direct:

	£
Grant	45,000
Catering	6,750
Donations (50%)	8,500
Insurance Services (50%)	8,000
Total Direct Income	68,250

Expenditure:

Direct Costs:

	£
Manager	22,000
Finance Assistant	10,000
Catering Assistant	10,000
Admin Support	7,500
Service Co-ordinators (50%)	10,000
Sessions (50%)	6,000
Volunteer Expenses (50%)	2,000
Office	2,000
Building (50%)	5,000
Total Costs	74,500

At the direct cost level the service will make a loss of £6,250, primarily due to the catering not covering the staff costs. In addition there are management overhead costs of £20,899. Should ACCT therefore ask the Council for a larger grant and, if so, for how much?

Exercise 5.6 – version 2

Have the overhead costs been correctly apportioned? The director, finance and catering managers' time have a direct cost element to ACCT. This should be allowed for, before apportionment should take place. The director proposed that they and the other managers be paid 10 per cent extra for responsibility and time. If we take out the direct costs before the 10 per cent responsibility allowance of the catering manager's time as cook (£12,000); the director as manager (£25,000) the finance officer (£20,000) this is £57,000. The revised management overhead is therefore £62,700 – £57,000 = £5,700. This is the cost, which should be allocated on a service level criteria/225 places. Therefore costs are £25.33p (£5,700/225) per place. The new service should therefore have management costs of £1,900 (£25.33 x 75) and CT management costs are now £3,800. Adopting a cost centre approach for the new organisation would give the following projected budget:

	Urban Centre	ACCT	Total
Income	£	£	£
Council grant	45,000	80,000	125,000
Catering	6,750	13,500	20,250
Donations	8,500	17,000	25,500
Insurance/services	8,000	16,000	24,000
Total Income	68,250	126,500	194,750

Expenditure

	£	£	£
Direct Costs	74,500	126,000	200,500
Overheads	1,900	3,800	5,700
Total Expenditure	**76,400**	**129,800**	**206,200**
Surplus (Deficit)	(8,150)	(3,300)	(11,450)

On this basis the organisation should negotiate on seeking an increase in grant to cover the deficit.

Chapter 6
charity accounts and financial management

> **Objectives: By the end of this chapter you should understand:**
>
> 1. The Statement of Recommended Practice for Charities
> 2. Audit and Independent Examination requirements for charities
> 3. How to interpret a set of published accounts.

INTRODUCTION

Charity accounting changed in the 1990s with the official recognition that charity operations were very different from commercial companies. Previously charities had produced Income and Expenditure accounts which, in essence, were the same as profit and loss accounts. In recognition of these differences – for example, the object of a charity is not to make a profit but to spend money on its charitable objectives – the Charity Commission set up a working party to help improve the quality of financial reporting by charities and to assist those who are responsible for the preparation of the charity's annual report and accounts. An agreed Statement of Recommended Practice for charity accounts, commonly known as the SORP, was published in October 1995 and subsequently revised in October 2000. Although the word 'recommended' is used, the SORP is actually in the main mandatory as it forms the basis of the accounting regulations prescribed in the 1993 Charities Act. Even for charities formed as companies it is seen as best practice.

Transparency

Non-incorporated charities above the threshold of £10,000 a year are subject to greater scrutiny and accountability than in the past. The responsibility of ensuring a charity is meeting its objective and properly running its affairs are the responsibilities of the trustees. Our starting point in understanding a charity's accounts is to recognise that the responsibility for the accounts is also that of the trustees. Secondly, the published accounts are not the auditor's or Charity Commission's accounts, they are the organisation's. There are many other groups interested for very different reasons in the published accounts: employees, volunteers and beneficiaries; funders and the general public; suppliers and lenders; and finally various government departments and agencies. *The Good Financial Management Guide* (pages 177-180) provides a comprehensive list of all those interested and why.

Thirdly, whereas figures are the essence of accounts, our starting point in understanding charity accounts is through words. The revised SORP places increased emphasis on the formal narrative in the trustees' report. The report now has to include information about the charity's objectives, activities and achievements and its policies in respect of reserves, investments and grant-making, as well as a commentary on the financial position of the charity and a risk statement.

The SOFA

The change which is probably the most radical of all is the introduction of a Statement of Financial Activities, popularly known as the SOFA. This essentially amalgamates the old income and expenditure account with the statement of gains/losses and the reconciliation and analysis of the movement of funds.

The main purpose of the SOFA is to bring together all transactions in a single statement so as to present a complete picture, which will give a true and fair view of the charity's financial activities during the year. It records all the charity's incoming resources, both revenue income and capital (endowments), and shows how they have been expended during the year. Essentially it combines an income and expenditure account with an analysis of the changes over the year in the different funds held by the charity. Care is needed to disclose all the transactions correctly in the restricted and unrestricted fund columns.

The layout is set out in the Regulations and must be followed. The minimum requirement for an endowed charity with multiple funds will normally be a column for unrestricted funds, one for restricted income funds and one for endowments. The revised SOFA also groups items of expenditure under standard headings – for example, 'Cost of Generating Funds' which includes fundraising and publicity. This functional classification of expenditure also means that the costs of the charity's activities are described by activities such as 'visit at home service' rather than rent, rates etc. In addition, there are other categories relating to 'support costs in furtherance of the objects of the charity', management and administration and 'costs of generating funds'. The Charities' SORP and guidance on these headings for those new to charity accounting is explained in Charity Commission guidance leaflets.

The different types of funds are explained in Chapter 4, Resource Management (page 110) of *The Good Financial Management Guide*.

PRINCIPLES OF FUND ACCOUNTING AND A STATEMENT OF FINANCIAL ACTIVITIES

SAMPLE EXERCISE

Exercise 6.1

You are the finance director of a new community organisation and you are asked to prepare the accounts at the end of the first year ending 31 December 2000. During the year the charity received and spent the following income:

1. Received £200,000 in respect of a contract restricted to develop a day care centre. In respect of this project you have incurred the following costs:

Salaries	£80,000
Travel to Site	£10,000
Licenses etc	£5,000
Total	£95,000

2. Received £50,000 in respect of a donation from a trust, which has given you the money towards the cost of running an advice service. Of this sum, £10,000 was spent by the project end.

3. General donations and covenanted income of £80,000 were received. From this the sum of £5,000 was spent on general activities.

4. You incurred running costs as follows:

Fundraising and publicity	£20,000
Management and administration	£30,000
Total	£50,000

5. Interest was earned on the unspent funds as follows:

Day Centre Contract	£5,000
Money from Trust	£2,000
General Donations	£3,000
Total	£10,000

ANSWER TO EXERCISE 6.1

Statement of Financial Activities
For the Year Ended 31 December 2000

	Unrestricted Funds £000	Restricted Funds £000	Total £000
Resources Arising:			
Donations	80	250	330
Interest earned	3	7	10
Total	83	257	340
Resources Used:			
Direct Charitable Expenditure:			
Day Care Project	0	95	95
Advice Centre	0	10	10
General Charitable Expenditure	5	0	5
Total	5	105	110
Other Expenditure:			
Costs of Generating Funds	20	0	20
Management and Administration	30	0	30
Total	50	0	50
Resources Used in Year	55	105	160
Net Incoming Resources	28	152	180
Net Movement of Funds	28	152	180

Balance Sheet as at 31 December 2000

	£000
Cash at Bank and in Hand	180
Funds:	
Restricted Funds	152
General Funds	28
	180

Guidance on the Statement of Recommended Practice on Accounting and Reporting by Charities (SORP 2000) is available from the Charity Commission and on the Internet at www.charity-commission.gov.uk

REGULATION

The 2000 Regulations/SORP detail the accounting and reporting requirements applicable to charities and are available from the same Charity Commission website.

For unincorporated charities the financial thresholds governing the type of accounts and what kind of external scrutiny is required are:

Annual gross income/ total expenditure	Type of accounts	Type of external scrutiny
Below £10,000	Receipts and payments option	None required
Above £10,000 but below £100,000*	Receipts and payments option	Independent examination option
Above £100,000 but below £250,000	Accruals mandatory	Independent examination option
Above £250,000	Accruals mandatory	Audit

* *gross income only*

In addition, charities with annual income of less than £1,000 and who do not have a permanent endowment or occupy premises of their own need not register with the Charity Commission. Those charities with annual income and expenditure of less than £10,000, i.e. the 'light touch' regime, need not submit a copy of their accounts to the Charity Commission unless they are specifically asked for them. All registered charities with an annual income in excess of £10,000 will have to submit a copy of their annual report and accounts to the Commission together with a completed Annual Return for monitoring purposes.

Independent examination is a less onerous form of scrutiny than audit, both in terms of the depth of work to be carried out and the qualification necessary to undertake such work. The examiner is not required to form an opinion as to whether the accounts show a true and fair view but reports instead, based on the examination carried out, whether reportable facts have come to his or her attention.

However, many charities will because of their own constitution/trust deed still require audit whatever their size. The audit rules applying to incorporated charities with an income under £250,000 are different, reflecting the lack of harmony between charity and company law. Incorporated charities with an income between £10,000 and £90,000 require no form of examination. Incorporated charities between £90,000 and £250,000 require an audit exemption report. All incorporated charities have to produce their accounts on the accrual basis and show a 'true and fair view' to comply with company law.

The charity legislation makes clear that auditors and independent examiners are required to report certain matters direct to the Charity Commission. The government believes that this obligation is essential to strengthen accountability and public confidence in charities. The Auditing Practices Board has given guidance on what constitutes material or significant matters, which an auditor should report to the Commission. This is to avoid small or insignificant matters being reported which should be handled in a management letter to the trustees.

The three main types of material or significant matter are:

1. A significant inadequacy in the arrangements made by trustees for the direction and management of a charity's affairs

> **ACTION POINTS FOR YOUR ORGANISATION**
>
> 'Audit' your organisation by checking to see:
>
> 1. What an external analyst would make of your accounts. Would a potential funder give you money? Look at the published accounts against the checklist
>
> 2. Whether your charity complies with the Regulations
>
> 3. If the management team understand the accounts – offer to run a training session on them
>
> 4. How the accounts are presented and explained to the chief executive and the trustees.

2. A significant breach of a legislative requirement in respect of the charity's trusts

3. Circumstances indicating a probable deliberate misuse of charity property.

INTERPRETING PUBLISHED ACCOUNTS

The following ten questions are a useful checklist to use when looking at a published set of accounts.

✓ ✗   1. Are restricted funds properly identified and explained?

✓ ✗   2. Are designated funds explained? Do you consider them definite commitments?

✓ ✗   3. Are fundraising costs properly identified?

✓ ✗   4. Are management and administration costs properly identified?

✓ ✗   5. Are the trading subsidiary (if applicable) activities properly identified?

✓ ✗   6. Do charitable expenditure headings properly describe the activity of the charity?

✓ ✗   7. Are income sources properly identified?

✓ ✗   8. Do the accounts show a surplus or a deficit?

✓ ✗   9. Is there a reserves policy?

✓ ✗   10. Any other issues?

WHAT HAVE WE LEARNT?

1. What type of external scrutiny does an incorporated charity with an income of £245,000 require?

2. List the material or significant matters an auditor must report to the Charity Commission.

3. Where do fundraising costs appear in the SOFA?

EXERCISE 6.2 TEST YOUR KNOWLEDGE OF THE SORP

Do try all the questions – circle the correct answers

1) Under the Charities Act 1993, charities must file their accounts with the Charity Commission within a specific number of months from their year-end, namely:

   (a) nine months
   (b) ten months
   (c) six months
   (d) None of the above?

2) The main obligation in preparing a charity's account is to show a true and fair view of its incoming resources, their application and its state of affairs; except in the case of:

   (a) small charities which elect to prepare a receipts and payments account
   (b) charitable companies
   (c) charities with branches
   (d) charities financed from permanent endowments?

3) An incorporated charity is promised a grant of £200,000 in the year to 31 March 1999 (the charity's year-end) for the salary costs. The grant was not received until May 1999. Actual income received in the year was £90,000. On what basis would the charity require to prepare its accounts for the year to 31 March 1999?

   (a) a receipt and payments basis and would require a reporting accountant's report
   (b) a receipt and payments basis and would require an audit
   (c) a full accruals accounting basis and would require a reporting accountant's report
   (d) a full accruals accounting basis and would require an audit.

4) The value of resources accruing to a charity should be recorded in the SOFA:

   (a) when the financial year ends
   (b) only when the cash has been received
   (c) as soon as it is prudent and practical to do so
   (d) even if the conditions for receipts have not been met?

5) An incorporated charity with income of £260,000 and assets of £5m will require:

   (a) an audit
   (b) an independent examiner's report
   (c) a report by a reporting accountant
   (d) no examination or report?

6) In respect of investment property owned by an unincorporated charity, which of the following statements is true?

   (a) it must be revalued professionally every year
   (b) it must be revalued professionally every five years
   (c) it must be revalued every year
   (d) none of the above.

7) Under the Charities Act 1993, which is the earliest year an unincorporated charity does not require a full audit?

Year	Income	Expenditure
	£	£
1	490,000	90,000
2	80,000	350,000
3	40,000	40,000
4	90,000	60,000
5	90,000	40,000
6	40,000	40,000
7	90,000	10,000

   (a) year 2
   (b) year 4
   (c) year 5
   (d) none of the above

8) Your charity has received a permanent endowment of £100,000. Half the money was invested in shares, which were worth £100,000 at the year-end and other half was left in the bank. Income received from the shares amounted to £5,000 (including tax credit) and gross bank interest received was £5,000. How much was the endowment fund balance at the year-end?

   (a) £90,000
   (b) £150,000
   (c) £155,000
   (d) £160,000

9) A charity is given a cottage as part of a legacy – probate value £100,000. The legacy was intended by the legatee to provide an income for the charity. The charity decides to use it as a holiday home and received rent of £30,000. The market value of the cottage was £130,000 at the year-end, based on its rental yield, but its insurance value was £125,000. The cottage has a useful life of ten years. At what value would it be included in the accounts at the year-end?

   (a) £90,000
   (b) £100,000
   (c) £125,000
   (d) £130,000

10) A charity has two funds: a general fund of £10,000, and a restricted fund of £40,000. The charity invested the funds in the same deposit account and earned interest of £5,000. The trustees decided to set up a designated fund with £5,000 of the unrestricted fund. What would be the total of the unrestricted funds held at the end of the period?

(a) £5,500
(b) £10,000
(c) £11,000
(d) £15,000

11) If the amount is substantial, how should help received by a charity from volunteers be disclosed in the accounts?

(a) no disclosure necessary
(b) included in the SOFA in the same way as gifts in kind
(c) included in the SOFA if the charity would otherwise have paid staff for the same work
(d) not included in the accounts but referred to in the notes or trustees' report.

12) Under the Charities Act 1993 it states that the accounting records must:

(a) show the solvency of the charity at any time
(b) show the financial position at any point in time
(c) disclose the financial position at the end of the financial year
(d) be written up on a daily basis to show the current financial position?

13) A non-incorporated charity, expects income of £30,000 for the year ended 31 March 1999 and has had this level of income for the last five years. In the past it had an audit because its trust deed required an audit and the trustees thought it was necessary. When can this charity take advantage of the new charity regulations to avoid the cost of audit?

(a) only after changing the trust deed
(b) as soon as the trustees inform the existing auditors
(c) immediately
(d) as soon as the existing auditors have resigned.

14) In response to an appeal, your charity has received a gift of shares worth £20,000 and cash of £50,000 to be used for relief in Cuba. During the year the shares have produced income of £15,000 and the sale of 50 per cent of the shares generated proceeds of £25,000. At the end of the year the charity spent £60,000 on Cuba. How much is the fund balance at the year-end?

(a) £30,000
(b) £35,000
(c) £40,000
(d) £45,000

15) A non-incorporated charity prepares its accounts on a receipts and payments basis to the 31 March 1998. It received £95,000 in the year. In addition it has claimed back tax credits of £10,000 on its dividends. This money was received after the year-end. Assume that the trustees do not wish to change the basis of accounting unless this is required. In this case, the accounts should disclose:

(a) income of £95,000 and be prepared on a receipts and payment basis
(b) income of £105,000 and be prepared on a receipts and payment basis
(c) income of £105,000 and be prepared on an accruals basis
(d) either income of £95,000 or £105,000 depending on whether the tax refund is received before the accounts are approved?

16) A small charity producing a receipts and payments accounts:

(a) need not distinguish restricted funds from general funds
(b) may produce a statement of assets and liabilities instead of a balance sheet
(c) must file their accounts within nine months of the financial year-end
(d) must have the accounts independently examined?

17) A charity sells donated goods through its subsidiary which raised income of £100,000 and shop expenses were £40,000 giving a profit of £60,000. The charity's consolidated Statement of Financial Activities should show:

(a) income of £100,000 under trading income
(b) income of £100,000 under donations
(c) net profit of £60,000 as a single line
(d) none of the above?

ANSWERS TO EXERCISE 6.2

1) b
2) a
3) d
4) c
5) a
6) c
7) c
8) b
9) d
10) c
11) d
12) b
13) a
14) c
15) a
16) b
17) b

Chapter 7
tax and voluntary organisations

> **Objectives: By the end of this chapter you should understand:**
>
> 1. The importance of tax planning for charities
> 2. Principles of VAT applicable to charities
> 3. Methods of tax-efficient giving to charities.

INTRODUCTION

With careful planning a charity will not have to pay any direct taxation (income/corporation tax). Furthermore a charity can maximise resources by taking advantage of the many concessions in indirect tax (VAT) available to charities and using the incentives for effective giving (i.e. gift aid). This chapter is primarily concerned with VAT and tax-effective giving. But first a brief word on direct tax and to dispel the myth that charities are automatically exempted from paying direct tax. As Randall and Williams point out, legislation – the Income and Corporation Taxes Act – affecting charities starts with the important point that :

> '... exemptions are not granted automatically ... they are granted only on a claim. This claim will need to be supported by evidence, or granted on proof before the Commissioners for special purposes, as the 1842 Act put it. For the proof to be acceptable the claim must relate to income solely applicable for charitable purposes, and actually applied for charitable purposes.'

Deciding whether an organisation is charitable or not is now the responsibility of the Charity Commission in England and Wales (in Scotland, the Revenue still makes this decision) and the Revenue will normally automatically grant relief to registered charities. However, problems can sometimes arise for a charity when its circumstances change – for example, sources of income or how money is spent – which can mean that the Revenue may require additional assurances that reliefs can still be applied or, if not satisfied, they can be withdrawn. Legislation governing the granting of reliefs operates by the use of five concepts:

- Relevant income and gains
- Qualifying expenditure
- Non-qualifying expenditure
- Total income
- Non-taxable income.

Most charities do not pay income tax but the charity finance director should be aware of these direct taxation issues and compliance with Revenue regulations on paying staff and consultants. Charities need to take considerable care if the organisation involves itself in trading activities and decides to set up a trading subsidiary. A business plan needs to be prepared and appropriate professional advice taken.

UNDERSTANDING VAT

The Good Financial Management Guide (Chapter 7) is devoted to understanding tax. In summary:

Commercial organisations usually charge VAT on the goods or services they supply and will pay VAT on the products etc they buy in. VAT is a tax on turnover, not on profit. Registered traders may therefore deduct the tax which they incur on supplies to them (input VAT) from the tax they charge to their customers (output VAT). The balance, i.e. the value added, is then paid over to Customs and Exercise. VAT is a tax on sales, which is built upon the principle that the final consumer is the one to bear the tax.

Voluntary organisations suffer a number of problems when it comes to VAT. First they incur VAT costs on supplies they buy in. Secondly, income for the majority of voluntary sector organisations is outside the scope of VAT, e.g. donations, legacies, investment income. Only income (for example sponsorship) which is liable to VAT can be used to be setoff for VAT on supplies brought in. Because of this, for the vast majority of voluntary organisations VAT is a genuine expense and is commonly referred to as 'irrecoverable VAT'. However, as *The Good Financial Management Guide* states:

'One objective of financial management is to minimise the amount of irrecoverable VAT; this can usually be done by taking maximum advantage of the VAT reliefs available when supplies are made to charities and by planning, for example, fundraising and the provision of services in a way that minimises the risk of such activities being liable to VAT.'

VAT is charged on taxable supplies of goods and services by a taxable person. The term person includes individuals, partnerships, trusts, companies and charities. If a person is making taxable supplies, then the value of these supplies is called the taxable turnover. If a person's taxable turnover exceeds certain limits, known as the registration threshold (for the current threshold check with your local VAT office or accountants) then they are a taxable person and should be registered for VAT. For charities a good rule to follow in defining whether activities fall within VAT or not is to assume business activities as falling within the scope of VAT and non-business activities as falling outside its scope. However, if in any doubt take professional advice. A taxable supply is a supply of goods and services other than an exempt supply. A taxable supply is either standard rated – currently 17.5 per cent or zero rated at 0 per cent – or exempt which means that the supply is not chargeable to VAT.

The following example illustrates the differences:

Charity:	A	B	C
	Standard Rated	Zero Rated	Exempt Rated
	£	£	£
Inputs	80,000	80,000	80,000
VAT	14,000	14,000	14,000
Outputs	120,000	120,000	120,000
VAT	21,000	0	0
Pay (reclaim)	7,000	(14,000)	0

Zero rated means that no VAT is chargeable, but a registered person may recover the input on related expenses (as charity B). In addition, voluntary organisations may make supplies that are zero rated. These include books, periodicals and other publications, certain aids designed for use by handicapped persons, the sales of donated goods and distribution of goods overseas. Voluntary sector income which is outside the scope of VAT includes:

- Donations, legacies and bequests

- Funds raised for no return (i.e. sponsored walks) but not sales or admission fees

- Grants from public funds, provided they are not in return for services

- Dividends from equities (but not bank deposit interest and other loan interest which is technically exempt)

- Trading of equities (only where a charity is concerned; otherwise it would be exempt).

Exempt supplies include youth club services, welfare services, education, research, vocational training, health and financial services.

VAT planning and maximising recovery

Tax planning is important for voluntary organisations and particularly registered charities. Organisations which are not compulsorily required to register for VAT may still consider doing so under what is called voluntary registration. This is because it may allow a partial recovery of VAT incurred.

Such a decision requires being able to answer the following questions:

- Will the VAT the organisation is able to recover exceed that which it will have to declare to Customs on standard rated activities?

- Will the organisation's 'customers' be able to bear the cost of VAT that will now be charged? (This should not be a problem for commercial organisations.)

- Will the costs of setting up the financial system to record and claim VAT be covered?

Voluntary organisations should always be seeking to recover as much VAT as possible. Because voluntary organisations have a mixture of supplies that are tax exempt and outside the scope, there are issues as to how much of their costs can be recoverable and how much is irrecoverable. Issues particularly around the expenses attributable to head offices where some of these costs can be recovered require careful planning and negotiation with Customs and Exercise. Professional advice from a specialist charity VAT expert may be required. This does not mean the charity has to incur direct fees. Many firms of accountants with specialist charity departments have charity VAT experts who will base their fee as a percentage of the amount of VAT they can recover and will also cap their fees to an agreed amount, as the following case study demonstrates.

CASE STUDY 7.1

A charity whose objectives included the funding of research and provision of welfare to children who had a particular disease had remained unregistered for VAT since its formation. The taxable income it generated had been historically low, as its main sources of income were research grants (outside the scope), donations and legacies (outside the scope) and fundraising activities (mainly exempt). The opportunity to register for VAT arose when it decided to open a charity shop selling goods donated by the public (specifically zero rated). The shop was very successful and soon the charity had five shops with a turnover of £250,000.

On speaking with professional charity VAT advisors, VAT registration was sought retrospectively from the date the first shop was opened (retrospective voluntary registration can be sought up to three years from the date of application). This ensured all VAT incurred during this period attributable to the shops to be fully recovered and a healthy proportion of overhead VAT. In addition, all VAT incurred on the annual ball and other fundraising events was fully recoverable as it fell below the partial exemption de minimis limits.

The charity enjoyed a one-off windfall of £75,000 and further an enduring annual VAT recovery of circa £12,000. As the majority of taxable income is zero rated there is little VAT to pay on income. The professional advisors charged a one-off fee of ten per cent of the windfall received plus VAT (which was fully recoverable!).

Charity taxation and, in particular, VAT is a complex subject. It is also constantly changing, for example, VAT on advertising. As from 1 April 2000, recruitment adverts and the costs of preparing them became zero rated for VAT purposes, along with other advertising time and space brought by charities. *The Good Financial Management Guide* chapter on this subject provides a series of answers to the most popularly asked questions which the NCVO HelpDesk receives. In addition it provides some useful appendices including a VAT registration checklist and a glossary of common VAT terms.

TAX RELIEF ON GIVING

There are a number of ways individuals and companies can give to charities, which are tax efficient. In the 2000 budget new measures were announced that were designed to 'Get Britain Giving'. The principal methods of tax-efficient giving are:

1. Gift aid

Established in 1990 this particular method has seen the most radical change. Gift aid provides a way for individuals and companies to get tax relief on one-off donations of money. Previously there was a minimum amount of £250 that had to be paid. This has now been abolished. For individuals tax relief will be allowed on any donation, large or small, regular or one-off, provided it is made by a person who gives the charity a gift aid declaration. It also removes the requirement that the donor pay basic rate income tax equal to the tax deducted from the donation. Instead, there will be a requirement that the donor pay an amount of income tax or capital gains tax, whether at the basic rate or some other rate, equal to the tax deducted. This is intended to make the gift aid scheme suitable for many donors who pay income tax at a rate below the basic rate, or who pay capital gains tax. In addition, gift aid declarations can also be made through the Internet or orally over the phone. For corporate giving the process has been simplified. Companies pay their donations gross and do not have to make a gift aid declaration. Charities no longer have to reclaim any tax.

2. Deeds of covenants

The old system of covenants has now been brought under the new gift aid schemes. Existing deeds of covenant will stand in place of the gift aid declaration until the deed expires.

3. Payroll giving

Payroll giving schemes (or 'Give As You Earn') were introduced in 1986. Under such schemes employees can have their donation deducted from their gross salaries by their employer, who then pass the money on to an authorised agency (e.g. the Charities Aid Foundation) which in turn can pass it on to the charity. There is no need to reclaim the tax by the agency or the charity as the donation is made gross out of the employee's income before tax.

Administratively, therefore, this is very efficient for a charity. Previously there was an upper limit for payroll giving of £1,200 but this has now been abolished. Also from April 2000 and for the next three years the Government is supplementing donations made by an additional 10 per cent via the payroll giving agencies.

4. Other methods

There are various other methods and schemes by which individuals and companies can tax efficiently give to charities relating to capital. Within this category are reliefs relating to legacies and inheritance tax relief but this area is outside the brief of this manual. Only capital gains tax relief on a 'no gain, no loss basis' used to apply to donating quoted securities such as shares. Now income tax relief is given at the market value of the shares on the date of the gift. Individuals claim the relief in their tax return. Companies can also make charitable gifts of shares in other companies and claim relief against their profits for corporation tax purposes.

The advantages of tax-efficient giving require the finance director to be proactive in the organisation in briefing the fundraisers on technical implications and, if necessary, actively participating in explaining to companies or individuals.

EXERCISE 7.2 – APPRAISING A CHARITY'S TAX POSITION

In this exercise we review a charity's operations from the perspective of reducing the burden of tax. Direct taxation implications are discussed first. The answer then appraises the indirect tax position.

Wretched of the Earth is a charitable trust that was registered in 1962. Its purpose is to relieve poverty, distress and suffering in any part of the world. The charity operated from a building just off Soho Square, which was donated to it 15 years ago. On the ground floor, there is a 'restaurant' which offers frugal meals supposed to replicate the inadequate nourishment suffered by much of the world's poor. The restaurant is surprisingly popular, many of its clientele being overweight workers in the media industry located nearby.
The charity was formerly a quiet operation, which had concentrated on convincing the Overseas Development Agency (ODA) to give it a grant. Now, however, Harry Flashpoint, who was brought in by the trustees to give the charity a higher profile, runs it. Harry feels that his conspicuous lifestyle should be partly funded by the charity because the charity is benefiting.
On Friday nights, there is a 'rave for the poor' at the charity's premises. This has become massively popular due to the presence of trendy disc jockeys and various glitterati. The very high entrance fee means that only those with a large disposal income can get in, which increases the exclusiveness of the event.
    Part of the premises is used by the charity as a shop, from which goods made by artisans in Africa are sold, together with donated goods and a small range of bought-in-jewellery.

The charity's income expenditure for 2000/2001 was as follows:

INCOME	£
Collecting tin donations	1,500
ODA grant	227,000
Other donations	7,000
Legacies	12,000
Net profit on restaurant	75,700
Net profit on raves	125,000
Proceeds of sale of donated goods	12,000
Net proceeds of artisan goods	500
Net proceeds of bought-in goods	7,500
Total Income	468,200

EXPENDITURE	£
Setting up irrigation project	200,000
Costs of shop	8,000
Central charity administration	40,000
Clothes, meals for Harry	50,000
Rolls Royce hire for Harry	16,000
Harry's salary	50,000
Total Expenditure	364,000
Surplus	104,200

Question
What is the organisation's tax position?

ANSWER TO EXERCISES

Exercise 7.2

Wretched of the Earth

A) Direct tax

1. Charity has trading activities: restaurant
shop, bought-in goods
raves

These activities will probably be taxable. A possible answer to rectify the situation would be to set up a trading company which gift aids its profits. Are the trading activities profitable? From the information supplied the relevant income is:

	£
Restaurant profit	75,700
Raves	125,000
Bought-in goods	7,500
Artisan	500
	208,700

Issues of direct expenditure and the allocation of overheads as previously discussed in this guide would then have to be considered and a business plan drawn up.

B) Indirect tax

VAT treatment of income and expenditure:

Income

Collecting tin donations	OS
ODA grant	OS
Other donations	OS
Legacies	OS
Restaurant turnover	SR
Entrance fee to raves	SR
Proceeds of donated goods at shop	ZR
Sales of artisan goods	SR
Sales of bought-in goods	SR

Expenditure

Setting-up of irrigation project	OS
Costs of shop	SR
Central charity administration	SR
Clothes, meals for Harry	SR
Rolls Royce hire for Harry	SR
Harry's salary	OS

Code

EX = Exempt

OS = Outside the scope of VAT

SR = Standard rated

ZR = Zero rated

Other points

This standard-rated trading activity, if its turnover exceeds the new allowance in the Finance Act 2000 (maximum £50,000), will have to be put in a VAT-registered trading subsidiary to avoid income tax. If possible, as much of the input tax on administration should be put through the subsidiary for recovery of VAT.

> **ACTION POINTS FOR YOUR ORGANISATION**
>
> Audit your organisation to see if:
>
> 1. It is maximising VAT recovery. For example: When was the last time the organisation had professional advisors assessing the tax position of the organisation?
>
> 2. The trading subsidiary is profitable and keeping to its business plan
>
> 3. The fundraisers are fully briefed on tax-effective giving
>
> 4. The fundraising department have plans for maximising tax-effective giving among the charity supporters
>
> 5. The Charity's fundraising material is not creating a tax liability or restricting funds in an appeal.

WHAT HAVE WE LEARNT?

Questions: Answers are in the text or in the GFMG. Have a go before looking at them.

1. Name the five concepts governing the granting of reliefs.

2. What is a taxable person?

3. Define standard rate, zero rate and exempt.

4. List which voluntary sector income sources are outside the scope of VAT.

5. What factors need to be considered in deciding whether VAT voluntary registration is appropriate?

EXERCISE 7.3

St Mungo's Monastery is located just outside Eastry in Kent and was established in the late nineteenth century with a number of endowments from a wealthy individual. It is a registered charitable trust.

The monks are subject to the disciplines of the Order of the Sacred Veil and are not generally allowed out of the monastery. They are a very active bunch, engaged in a number of activities to keep their minds from sin. The monastery owns a vineyard that produces 'tonic' wine which is unusually strong and very popular. The monastery owns a large acreage, some of which has been turned over to market gardening, again carried out by monks. They also run a residential home for the elderly gentlemen (who are not monks) attached to the monastery. There is also a public house, The Laughing Abbot, owned by the monastery but staffed by outsiders. All the activities of the monastery are carried out by the charitable trust.

Income and expenses are as follows:

	£
Local authority contract for residential home	500,000
Set-aside funds from the European Commission	75,000
Grant from the local authority	120,000
Sale of bar meals in the pub	65,000
Sale of drinks in the pub	250,000
Hire of rooms for functions	15,000
Collections at services in the monastery church	175,000
National Lottery grant for repair of church	200,000
Monks' salaries donated	350,000
DSS Income Support and State pensions of elderly gentlemen	91,000
Sale of wine to wholesalers	1,200,000
Sales of produce from market garden to supermarkets	750,000
Monks' salaries paid	330,000
Salaries to full-time outsiders	510,000
Wages of part-time staff	60,000
Payments to freelancers and consultants	145,000
Redundancy payment to outsider	40,000
Repairs to church	300,000
Business rates	34,000
Council tax	6,250
Various materials used in manufacture of wine	350,000
Living expenses of monks	55,000
Donation to archdiocese	150,000
Advertising of tonic wine	30,000
Fundraising from bazaars, jumble sales etc	133,000

The part-time staff is paid out of petty cash with no reductions for income tax or National Insurance. At least one of the so-called freelance staff has duties that hardly differ from an employee.

Questions

1. The Inland Revenue is planning to visit the charity to ensure that PAYE has been properly deducted. What precautions should be taken by the charity?

2. State how the VAT system would treat each of the monastery's activities.

3. What recommendations would you make in relation to the monastery's activities in order to reduce liability to pay direct taxes?

ANSWERS

Answer to exercise 7.3

1) What precautions should be taken if an Inland Revenue PAYE audit is imminent?

Part-time staff
Depending on the level of pay, part-time staff should have income tax and NICs deducted in just the same way as full-time staff. A calculation should be made of the liability going back as far as necessary if tax and NICs have not been properly deducted. This is a liability of the charity, not employees. Penalties amounting to a maximum of the tax/NIC may also be payable, which cannot properly be borne by the charity and so must fall on its trustees personally. These will reduce depending on the level of co-operation with the Revenue, so be co-operative. Proper pay deduction records should be maintained from now on, and the correct form issued at the end of the tax year.

Form P46 (or P38S for students) should be signed by each part-time employee and retained for the Revenue to inspect.

Freelancers and consultants
The Revenue will endeavour to treat as many of these as employees as they can, so evidence of the proper self-employed status of each should be sought. If in doubt they should be treated as an employee and subjected to the PAYE scheme. This will upset the consultant but this is less damaging than using charity funds to pay their tax/NICs. The Revenue will use the following tests:

1. Control and work performance
Employees will not be able to decide in general where, when and how the work is performed. Self-employed have the power of delegation and do not have to work certain hours.

2. Financial risk
Employees do not risk their own personal capital if the work is not up to standard.

3. Equipment
Employees do not usually use their own equipment to carry out the work.

4. Holidays and sickness
Self-employed do not get these.

5. Exclusivity
In general, employees will work for the one employer. Not so with the self-employed.

If the Revenue has granted the particular consultant self-employed status and issued a 'Schedule D number' this should be obtained but it is not conclusive evidence.

Redundancy payment
This should be non-contractual. Care needs to be taken in this area for the payment to qualify for the £30,000 exemption. The remainder of it is taxable and tax should be deducted under PAYE. Any *ex gratia* payment will be a breach of trust, unless consent is obtained from the Charity Commission.

2) State how the VAT system would treat the monastery's activities.

Local authority contract for the residential home	EX
Set-aside funds from the European Commission	OS
Grant from the local authority	OS
Sale of bar meals in the pub	SR
Sale of drinks in the pub	SR
Hire of rooms for functions	SR
Collections at services in the monastery church	OS
National Lottery grant for repair of church	OS
Monks' salaries donated	OS
DSS Income Support and State pensions of elderly gentlemen	OS
Sale of wine to wholesalers	SR
Sale of produce from market garden to supermarkets	SR
Monks' salaries	OS
Salaries to full-time outsiders	OS
Wages of part-time staff	OS
Payments to freelancers and consultants	*see note 1*
Redundancy payment to outsider	OS
Repairs to church	SR
Business rates	OS
Council tax	OS
Various materials used in manufacture of wine	SR
Living expenses of monks	SR
Donations to archdiocese	OS
Advertising of tonic wine	SR
Fundraising from bazaars, jumble sales etc	EX

Note 1. Depends on whether the consultants are registered for VAT

```
           Code
   EX  = exempt
   OS  = outside the scope of VAT
   SR  = Standard rated
   ZR  = Zero rated
```

3) What recommendations would you make in relation to the monastery's activities and direct taxes?

A trading subsidiary should be established. The trust deed should be checked to see whether to invest in such a subsidiary would be *ultra vires*. The deed may need adjusting and this should be cleared with the Charity Commission.

If the subsidiary is to be financed partly by loan capital the loan should be properly documented and treated as if it was on an arm's length basis, with security, interest and repayment terms made explicit.

If the following activities remain in the charity they will become taxable, (unless they can be classed as 'ancillary') as D case I profits unless they fall within the Revenue's exemptions for small traders because they are not for the primary purpose of the charity, advancement of religion:

- Running of the pub and hire of rooms
- Production and sale of wine
- Sale of farm produce
- Running of residential home.

Other points

The VAT regulations should be complied with. The trading subsidiary will be making the taxable supplies and VAT should be accounted for on the normal basis. Record-keeping rules should be complied with.

The residential home has exempt income and any input VAT relating to this activity is not reclaimable.

References, further reading and sources of information

References:

Bashir, H (1999). *The Good Financial Management Guide.* NCVO Publications

Harrison, J. *Managing Charitable Investments.* ICSA Publishing

Hind, A. (1995). *The Governance and Management of Charities.* Voluntary Sector Press

Osbourne, S. (1996). *Managing in the Voluntary Sector.* International Thomson Business Press

Further reading:

There are now some excellent books on voluntary sector finance. It is also worth being on at least one of the accounting firms/investment firms' charity mailing lists to get regular newsletters and updates on issues such as the budget and how it affects charities.

Books covering a variety of charity finance topics:

Wise, D. (1998). *Accounting and Finance for Charities.* ICSA Publishing

Charity Finance Yearbook (2000). Charity Finance Directors Group. Plaza Publishing Limited

Moss, G (1999). *Banking,* Directory of Social Change

Sayer, K (1998). *A practical guide to financial management for charities,* Directory of Social Change

Specifically on the charity SORP – though with the recent changes, make sure you have the new editions:

Dawes, R G. *Charity Accountability and Compliance.* Butterworth's Tolleys

Randall A. *SORP and the Regulations: A Comprehensive Guide.* ICSA Publishing

Sayer, K. *A Practical Guide to accounting by Charities: New Accounting regulations and the revised SORP.* Directory of Social Change

Legal issues:

Bates, Wells & Braithwaite and Centre for Voluntary Sector Development. (2000). *The Fundraiser's guide to the Law*. CAF

Harland, S, Walker, L (Apr 2000) *Guide to the major trusts 2000/2001: Volume 3*. 2000/2001 Edition, Directory of Social Change

Reason J, Hayes R, Forbes D. (2000) *Voluntary but not Amateur*. LLVSC

Ticher P. (2000) *Data Protection for Voluntary Organisations*. Bates, Wells & Braithwaite

Charity taxation:

VAT Guide for voluntary organisations, 4th edition. (2001) NCVO

Cairns E. (1998) *Fundraising for Charity: A guide to taxation and the law*. Tolley

Sayer, K (1995) *A practical guide to PAYE for charities*. Directory of Social Change

General charity management:

The Good Employment Guide for the Voluntary Sector. (1999) NCVO

Adirondack S. (1998) *Just about Managing*. London Voluntary Service Council

Bruce, I. *Meeting Need, Successful Charity Marketing*. (1999) ICSA Publishing

Hudson M. (2000) *Managing without Profit*. Penguin

Reports:

Dimensions of the Voluntary Sector 2000 – 3 volumes. CAF

Directory of American Grantmakers that fund charitable organizations and individuals outside the USA. (2000). Chapel & York

Smyth, J. (Apr 2000) *Guide to UK Company Giving*. Directory of Social Change

Sources of voluntary sector statistical material, which are essential for strategic analysis.

UK Voluntary Sector Almanac (2000) NCVO

Charity Commission Annual Report

Magazines:

Voluntary Sector

NGO Finance

Charity Times

Third Sector

Professional Fundraising

Academic journals, which cover charity finance, particularly reporting on research:

Financial Accountability and Management. Blackwells

Public Money. CIPFA

Managerial Auditing Journal. MCB University Press

Journal of Non-profit and Voluntary Sector Marketing. Henry Stewart Publications

Websites:

If you have access to the Internet, websites are also worth visiting both on individual charities and

Charity Commission: www.charity-commission.gov.uk

NCVO: www.ncvo-vol-org.uk